It's About the People, Stupid!

A Customer Service Manual for Self Defense

by

Francis M. Murphy

&

Sidney C. Hurlbert

Linus
Publications, Inc.

Published by Linus Publications, Inc.

Deer Park, NY 11729

ISBN 1-934188-14-X

Printed in the United States of America.

10 9 8 7 6 5 4 3 2 1

DEDICATION

This book is dedicated to the families of Fran Murphy and Sidney C. Hurlbert, especially their parents, who raised them in a way that made this accomplishment inevitable. The authors would also like to thank Joyce Orrico for her dedicated work and support, which helped the authors create this book, and John Fallacco who helped to edit the volume and Deborah Allen who was its first reader.

TABLE OF CONTENTS

PART I

PART II

## CHAPTER 1

Introduction

Customers! Can't they be annoying? People in the trenches often tell us customers are becoming demanding each year. They list customers as inconsiderate, stubborn, difficult, and, even, rude.

Principals of schools often say "If it were not for those irritating students and parents, schools would be fun."

The problem is, without those annoying customers, none of us would be in business.

It is easy to blame the customer. But if the principals above were honest, they'd also have to exclude the teachers, staff, coworkers, the superintendent and the Board before schools would truly become fun for them. Chances are, however, these "customers" might have to remove the principal, too, to have fun.

The Pennsylvania Dutch expression, "I often wonder about people except thee and me, and sometimes I wonder about thee," comes to mind.

Many teachers assert, "If only these two kids were gone from this class, teaching would be great." Some research was done in the schools about removing the two problem students from the teachers' classes. What happened was that two more students emerged, as the "problem students", in the teacher's mind. It seems we all need to have, at least, a short list of "problem people" among our customers, perhaps to ensure that we, ourselves, do not become the "problems". If it weren't for these "problem people", perhaps we would be our colleague's problem.

We can view all kinds of people as annoying, not just customers but family, coworkers and our bosses. (Maybe, especially our bosses) A college registrar used to tell students that if they simply followed his written directions, that they would never have to see him. "That," he said, is what we are striving for." Imagine!

Many of us choose to have lives guided by our annoyance with other people. People can choose to be annoyed or to be delighted. Within tolerances, we are probably all surrounded by the same percentage of truly annoying people. Yet some of us laugh, have fun, and celebrate, most days, while others mope and moan. It appears to be our choice. Those of us who live lives filled with disappointment about other people harbor low expectations for other people. Research reveals time, and time again, that people will always rise to, or fall to, the expectations that others have for them.

Many experts in the field of customer relations assert there are three important reasons to focus on customer relations:

1. Positive customer relations improve the retention rate of customers. (This is true.)

2. Positive customer relations lead to "word of mouth" advertising. (This is also true.)

3. Positive customer relations can lead to greater profitability in the "for profit" sector, and greater effectiveness in the "non profit" sector. (Also true.)

This kind of motivation, however, does not drive front line employees. As anxious as employees are for the company to succeed, it does not get them out of bed in the morning or put a skip in their step, typically.

No. World-class customer relations brings fun to the workplace, and fun retains and motivates employees. Fun is infectious. Fun drags customers in and sets a continuing expectation for future behavior.

The best way for a manager to diagnose the morale of her organization is to ask every employee at every encounter, "Are you having fun?" If the answer is yes, follow up questions, are rarely needed. Happy employees are more productive and receive higher ratings for productivity and better evaluations for job performance.

Customer service springs from optimism, respect for others and high expectations. Workplaces where fun is an organizing principle provide outstanding customer relations. Grim workplaces rarely excite customers.

It does not matter whether the organization is a free clinic, in an urban center, a fortune 500 organization, a school, or a tire shop. A climate that is fun and optimistic creates greater productivity and higher customer and job satisfaction.

This book will take fun seriously. It is organized in three parts:

1.	On a practical level, how do front line people provide good customer service?

2.	How do managers organize groups so that outstanding customer service happens?

3.	What are the organizing fundamental psychological principles that support world-class customer service?

World-class customer relations are intrinsic to the quality of the product or service. A management-consultant colleague, Larry Robinson, was a guest at a Ritz Carlton Hotel. He checked out of his room and worked, using his computer, quietly in the lobby while he waited for the hotel- provided airport limo.

The hotel must have announced the arrival of the limo but, deep in thought, Larry didn't hear the announcement. He glanced out at the hotel entrance, after a while, only to see the limo leaving. He stowed his computer, grabbed his bags and jogged after the limo down the street, knowing in his heart he had lost his opportunity to catch his plane.

Larry was muttering on his way back to the hotel, when a hotel gardener asked, "What seems to be the problem, sir?" Larry explained the problem, and the gardener guided him back to the lobby where the gardener addressed the front desk clerk. The gardener said, "Mr. Robinson is a guest at our hotel. He has missed his limousine. He needs to catch a plane. Please issue me $25".

The desk clerk expressed her regret that Larry had missed the plane. She immediately gave the gardener $25. The gardener walked Larry to the door, hailed a cab, helped Larry put his bags in the trunk and gave Larry $25. The gardener said, "Here is $25. You will need $20 to pay for the cab. The other $5 is yours to do with as you please. If the cab driver gives great service, perhaps you would give it to him. Have a nice flight back, Mr. Robinson."

Many things happened in that encounter. First, Mr. Robinson became a devoted Ritz Carlton customer, and, not surprisingly – so have the dozens of others who have heard the story. These individuals now have their own stories of outstanding customer service to add to the well established Ritz Carlton legacy.

Maybe, more importantly, in that moment of extraordinary customer service, the gardener and the person at the front desk each had a bright shining moment. They may have smiled the rest of the day remembering how they helped Larry. These smiles led, of course, to more customer service, which led to happy customers which.....

The Ritz Carlton is not an unusually high paying institution. It retains its customers and its employees.

Life should be filled with small acts of kindness. What, in life, is more fun than helping others, or bringing a smile to someone's face?

That is the heart of a world-class customer service program, and why the best reason to give customer service is that it is fun.

# # #

How do you behave in an elevator? Have you watched others as they walk up to call the elevator? They press the elevator button to go up. The button lights, broadcasting, that the elevator system has received the request. However, some press it again, and sometimes, again, and again, and again.

Some people come to a bank of elevators and press the button then the one across the hall, then the one at the next bank of elevators. They look at their watches, and press them all again.

It is as if the hurried button pushers believe there is a computer saying, in response, "That lady on the fourth floor is in a real rush. Send her our elevator extra quickly".

How else can the behavior be explained?

Are we sometimes in too much of a rush?

# # #

Serving others serves oneself

Did you ever watch the automotive duels between two cars poised to seize the "close in" parking space, near the mall, that the Toyota was abandoning? The drivers' eyes are steely and focused, their chins, thrust out. Their gas petal foot is poised, and twitching.

Have you seen the nice people leave their church, synagogue, or mosque after prayerful poise, only to enter their cars ready to extinguish a fellow parishioner who had the bad taste to try to get to the main road first?

How about, in the grocery line marked 10 items or less, how do you behave? Are you counting, impatiently the number of items in the person's cart in front of you? Are you hoping the cashier will catch the offending customer with eleven items, and send her away, clearing you for an immediate landing?

What is going on?

Would your life change if a distant relative gave you $27,000,000? Really, a $27,000,000 tax free gift. How would you handle a person with 12 items in front of you, then? Would the following fantasy be a possibility?

The man in front of you has twelve items, and is in the "10 items or less" lane. "Hello. Sir, I see you have 12 items," you say in a casual and supportive manner.

"Yes, I do."

"Do you need anything else? I would be very happy to hold your place in line while you search for any additional items you may need, or would like," you might say. "Don't worry about the cashier, sir. If he treats us badly, I will just buy the store and fire him. Take your time, sir. I have you covered," you wink conspiratorially .

Would it change, if you just were given $27,000,000? Could it change? This impatience and hurry that is at the heart of our rudeness might change if the time pressures driven by work and other factors were removed. Are you different on vacation? Does the heightened pace and stress of life in this fast lane increase the rudeness in our customers, and, perhaps in us?

Most of our customers, indeed, most of us, do not wake up in the morning hoping to find ways to be rude or abrupt to those around us.

Many of us do wake up in a hurry, however. The pace of our lives has changed. The forty-hour week really once was a cultural reality. People had evenings free, and uninterrupted weekends. Some even rested on Sundays. In many states and municipalities stores were closed on Sundays. It was a day of rest, not a day to catch up on the responsibilities we failed to accomplish in the other six days.

In those days, people report that they even had the time to pursue a quaint activity called dinner at home together with the family. Do we remember that, or is it another myth? A study indicated that one factor held common by winners of national merit scholarships was that they ate dinner at home around a table, uninterrupted, with their families.

Imagine? That means, by inference that most students don't.

As a person in contact with customers, should we lament this change in our society, and the subsequent increase in haste and rudeness, or should we do something about it? What do we owe our customers and ourselves? What is the moral imperative for our behaviors?

The most important reason to give quality customer service is because, you, the person in contact with the customer, will have more fun, and, so will your customer if you give world class, customer service.. Fundamentally, it is about fun.

If we do, maybe we and our customers will touch what is human in us.

When we serve others with optimism and dignity, our own enjoyment goes up. Would you like to help someone today? Of course. Who wouldn't? Altruistic people live longer. They report more happiness and more life satisfaction. More than one time, a nasty greedy person has "got the best" of one of your authors in some commercial dispute. It is not a difficult task, if you have no ethics. We always walk away saying, "At least I am not him."

# # #

Strive to reduce stress

Did you ever notice that when the stewardess or steward is giving you emergency directions prior to flight, they tell you that "in the unlikely event in a drop in cabin pressure, you need to pull that little clear tube tight and put the mask on yourself first? ..."

Why?

Don't they like children? No, that's not it. The reason? You can't help others put on a mask when you are unconscious from lack of oxygen, because you have failed to put on your mask. Take care of yourself first. Quality customer service occurs when you care about yourself. You can help yourself through an impulse to generosity.

Help yourself, live longer, be happier, be more productive, and have more friends, by helping other people.

Some statistics:

- 75% of visits to doctor's offices are stress related.

- Last year $400,000,000,000 was spent on stress related problems.

- Those people, who are overly stressed or troubled, have a 50% increased chance of serious illness or injury over their less stressed peers.

- 64% of marriages end in divorce, much of that, related to stress.

Stress takes a toll. Helping others (giving quality customer service) lowers stress.

Satisfying our impulse toward generosity is what others regard, in us, as heroism and it lowers our stress, increases profit, causes word of mouth advertising to go up, and increases repeat business.

Why do most of us believe that the quality of customer service is going down? A negative attitude affects customers and affects fellow employees.

"How are you today", Sid asked, cheerfully.

"Don't even go there. It's going to rain, sleet, or hail", the woman said.

What is going on here? Why are some people like that?

The little things

Sid likes to share this poem.

Remember Me

I am the fellow who enters the restaurant and patiently waits while the waitresses finish their conversations before taking my order.

I am the fellow who goes into the department store and waits patiently while the clerks finish their "chit-chat".

I am the guy who drives into the service station, who never blows my horn, and waits while the attendant takes his time.

You might say I am the good guy, but, you know who else I am? I am the guy who never comes back.

No one murders businesses; they just commit suicide on the backs of their disinterested employees.

# # #

Poor service has changed the syntax of our conversations. "Hi," Fran says on the telephone.

"Yes," comes the faceless reply.

(Since when is "yes" a reply to "hi?" The person on the other end doesn't want to take the time to greet me and ask me what I *want*. She compacts it all into one word, inappropriately placed.)

"Is Diane in", Fran continues.

"Just a minute", the voice replies.

(Since when is "just a minute" a reply to, "Is Diane in?")

The response of these receptionists is common. But, it is contemptuous of the language and of Fran.

# # #

At the hotel Sid greets the receptionist, "Hi".

"Reservations," the clerk asks. ("Reservations?" You bet! I have reservations about someone who won't answer a greeting with a greeting.)

"Yes, my name is Sid Hurlbert".

"We don't have you." ("You bet you don't, I'll never come here again.")

People either don't know, or they don't care how they come across.

How do you want to be treated? Sid asks this question at 200 seminars across the nation each year. The answers don't vary by 5 percent:

- "I want to be addressed promptly".

- "I want to be treated with respect."

- "I would like to be greeted with a smile."

- "I would like people to give me their undivided attention."

- "I would like people to treat me in a friendly way."

One time in Jamestown, New York a woman, in one of Sid's audiences, replied, "That she would like to be treated like a queen."

A man in the audience hollered out, "Hell, I just would like to be treated."

Treating people well is not a mystery. Yet, managers don't seem to, "Get it".

# # #

Sid use to go to a particular store in his hometown. There was a product there that he liked and at a price he thought was reasonable. The store was in a convenient location.

Yet, the people in the store didn't treat the customers well.

Sid always walked out with his product feeling abused. It wasn't that they were nasty. They just were not nice. The people stocking the shelves did not take time to look at him. The cashier did not greet him; and, she did not look at him when she gave him change. She always seemed to be engaged in a conversation with the cashier next to her, and was certainly, not focused on Sid, as a customer. The store was dirty. The displays were not thoughtful, or well lit.

As a kindness, Sid approached the manager. Sid asked if he could have a moment with the man.

The manager sighed, and looked at his watch, impatient that a customer would interrupt his day. Sid already knew where some of the problems came from. Don't you? Do people treat you this way sometimes, too?

He explained to the man that there was a particular product that he liked in the store, that the store was convenient, and that the price was right, but, "the customer service was just not up to par".

"And ...", the manager challenged Sid, as if to say , "And your point is?"

"It is just that I am a customer. I have been a customer here for years. I am thinking of not coming back because your customer service is so bad," Sid replied.

"Is that it?" the manager paused, glancing again at his watch. "That's where you are wrong. These people have all been trained in customer service and they are as good as you can get, these days. The new employees we hire are not like our generation."

The manager's behavior was fairly typical of a certain kind of manager. They would rather blame poor customer relations on their employees' character, than on their management and supervision techniques. For this man, the quality of the employees will always be bad. Sid was still unhappy and called the corporate office. He asked to speak to the customer relations person. He explained that he was a long time customer who regularly went to the store in that city to buy a particular product; that the price was fine; that the location was fine; but, he was thinking of stopping his business with the store because the customer service was not up to snuff.

The manager replied, "That's not true. I trained them myself."

Sid explained that he was a customer service trainer, and that he felt he might be able to help. The man declined. Sid asked, in a moment of inspiration, whether he could share a story with the man from the corporate office. "If at the end of this story you have not come to agree with me, I won't trouble you any more today."

"Just move it along," the manager replied, probably looking at his watch, too. Sid couldn't really tell that, on the phone, but he guessed that it was so.

"Imagine", Sid began, that I have come to visit your house. We are having a drink standing in front of the fireplace; a dog enters the room, walks up along side of us, and craps on the white carpet. In this story, you have two choices. The first choice is that you can say, 'Who is that dog. I never saw it before in my life. What is <u>he</u> doing in my house?' The second choice is you can say, 'That's my dog. I trained him myself."

Sid paused. The man sighed and said, "Is that it?"

"Well, yes," Sid said. "The people who work in that store are 'crapping' all over me."

"Maybe, that it is the way you tell it," the man replied. "I've got to get going now."

Sid does not shop at that store anymore. The store is continuing to go downhill. A new store, with a similar product line, has opened up in the town, sensing the opportunity. In time, the store with poor customer service will close. The employees will be laid off and when they close, the manager will be quoted in the local paper as stating that the reason the store closed was a declining economy in the region. Of course, all the former customers will know why it closed. Employees who have worked at that store for decades will lose their pension, and investors will lose their investment. The local economy will be disrupted and many families will suffer, in untold ways. But, the man from corporate "trained them himself".

##

It is always the little things that crash customer service. The things that bring companies down are tiny, but accumulated over time. Earlier in this section, we mentioned customers having to wait while the servers finished their conversation. Imagine you have entered the restaurant and have waited six or seven minutes to be attended to. Six or seven minutes is not a very long time, but most of us find it to be an eternity when waiting to be served. So, it has been six or seven minutes, and the servers are talking earnestly in the corner. while you quietly boil at your table.

Are there reasons for this apparent rude behavior on the part of the servers? There are always reasons. "It's not my table; Hilda's in the back, picking up a spill." Or, "It's only one more minute until the next shift comes in; We should not start to serve these people before the new shift arrives."

There are always reasons for inattention, or indifference to customers, but 68 percent of customers quit doing business with a company, primarily because of perceived indifference or no contact.

Phone customers report annoyance if the phone rings three or more times before they are attended to. Has any customer ever praised the dreaded phone menus, "Press two if you would like to...." Yet, look how those proliferated. Don't we know better?

It is always the little things.

## CHAPTER 2

The STEPS program represents a series of very basic principles for "front line" employees. (The people who deal directly with customers to improve customer relations.) The things that make a difference, in customer service, are small things. The consistent application of these principles make a huge difference, to you personally, and the success of the business.

They seem almost ridiculously simple but their consistent application will improve both morale and business.

Fundamental change is usually organized around basic principles. The STEPS program teaches very basic elements, choices really, that individual employees make in approaching their customers. Sid has been working with front line customer service representatives and the managers of these critical people for 30 years. It's simple: when organizations focus on these very simple principles, customer service has improved and profits have gone up. In the non-profit sector, customer loyalty has increased, and in both sectors, employee morale has improved.

What does the acronym STEPS stand for?

- S—Smile

- T—Tone of voice

- E—Expression/Facial

- P—Posture or body language

- S—Start putting into others what you want back

# # #

Take control of your attitude

Sid often asks his audiences, "How many of you want to have more fun?"

Not surprisingly, most people raise their hands to say they would like to have more fun. He then asks, 'How many of you would like to have your customers treat you better?" Again, most people raise their hands. And then, "How many of you would like to have your fellow employees treat you better?"

The answers are all obvious. Most of us want to be with people who have a great attitude. Most of us would like to surround ourselves with friends and families, for example, who are always ready for fun.

Most of us will settle for less, however. "Oh, her or him, sure, I would like to have a husband or wife with a better attitude but we have been married for 26 years." "Them, the kids? They don't have a great attitude either, but what are you going to do? We made them."

We should be more demanding about other peoples' attitude and that means we have to first take control of our own. Our positive attitude is the best way to influence others to have a positive attitude. What other tool do we really have to help others to lighten up?

Our attitude is a choice. That choice consistently influences the attitudes of everyone around us.

The world famous Seattle Pike Fish Market, retail outlet, has organized itself around four critical principles for success, one of which is, "Choose Your Attitude."

We can, and do, choose our attitude. Way too often, that choice is to our own detriment.

Fran is a regular volunteer at Camp Good Days and Special Times, a camp for challenged people. The camp supports childhood cancer victims, children of adults with cancer, the brothers and sisters of children with cancer, childhood AIDS victims, children, whose families have AIDS, childhood victims of abuse, children whose families have been affected by AIDS, and ...You get the idea.

Although Fran has served on the board and has volunteered in many of the programs that the camp offers, he is primarily associated with the childhood cancer camp. "It must be so sad," people often say to Fran when they hear of his volunteer work.

Of course.... it is not.

Children with cancer instinctively know they can choose their attitude. We are not sure how, or why, but they almost all seem to choose a great attitude. We all have a limited number of days on the planet. We can spend them as miserable, unhappy, grumpy people, dragging everyone else down around us, and having an exquisitely miserable time, or we can add to the planet's capacity for mirth.

Generally, at Camp Good Days, partially inspired by the generalized insanity of the staff and volunteers, kids with cancer are always laughing, and having a good time.

If these children can and do choose optimism over pessimism, and smiles over frowns; what is our responsibility for our choices, those of us, who are not being challenged with cancer? (At least, we hope you are not affected by cancer.)

We are faced with the choice, each day, of how we will relate to others. A poor choice will impact us most directly but will also bring everyone else down who we meet. A string of poor choices will directly lead to a miserable life.

# # #

Sid often laughs about his first trip across Wyoming. It was, he remembers, a very long state. He remembers three things about that very long drive:

1.   Grass.

2.   Antelopes

3.   A billboard which read, "Eat more lamb, a thousand coyotes can't be wrong."

Partly because Wyoming is so long, that billboard played over and over again in Sid's mind. He actually drove back to see if there was any fine print on the billboard. There was not. "Eat more lamb; a thousand coyotes can't be wrong." That was it. The point of the billboard was, apparently, to urge people to eat more lamb, using coyotes as experts about the taste of those rangy animals. But, Wyoming was long, so, Sid kept thinking about it (and chuckling).

Sid, to his credit, chuckles a lot. The way Sid thinks about that billboard, today, is that some things are obvious. Therefore, we don't talk about them, and; therefore, we miss the really simple things that can make a huge difference.

Don't miss what follows. It's obvious. It's simple. But, it will make all the difference on whether a business succeeds or fails; and, it will make the difference as to whether employees have fun on the job or dread going to work. It will make the difference as to whether your life is generally fun, or not.

# # #

S — Smile

The place to begin the STEPS program and to dramatically improve the customer relations for front line employees is they must smile. You should, too.

Don't smile all the time. (They will take you away and lock you up); but, do smile every time you make contact with another person. The Sprint Call Center has instituted a program to brighten the attitude of their employees. A supervisor was quoted as saying that she could hear the employees' smiles on the phone. Do you think you can hear a smile on the phone? Of course you can. A smile triggers a waterfall of physiological and psychological events. Physiologists have recorded that smiles can be very helpful. A smile accelerates the flow of blood and increases the oxygen to the brain. Smiles release endorphins that stimulate hundreds of other chemicals which generally improve our health.

Cancer patients, who are thought to be terminal, live longer, if they laugh more. Some hospitals have installed humor rooms for cancer patients. If the cancer patients laugh for two hours a day, studies have shown the patients both live longer and report higher satisfaction with the life they have to live.

We don't know about you, but, as for Sid and Fran, they would happily spend a few hours in a humor room to extend their lives and remain healthier, if they contracted cancer.

Once time when Sid was explaining this to a group, a man in the audience, familiar with the research said, "Yes, but that humor room only works for a certain percentage of cancer victims." I see, let's not endure the burden of laughter, because it might not extend every one of our lives.

Would you volunteer for the humor room if there was only an 80% chance of it extending your life and making you healthier? Would you volunteer for the humor room if there was only a 15% chance?

We would volunteer if there was not a chance. We might even volunteer if it slightly shortened our lives. Would you rather have 10 years smiling or 12 years frowning?

Sid is often asked, "Do you want me to smile even if I don't feel like it?", or:

"Do you want me to smile, even if it's insincere?"

Psychologists often puzzle over which causes what. Does the smile happen because you are happy, or can you become happy by smiling a lot? There is pretty good evidence that, if you change the behavior, the psychology behind it will also change. A smiling person soon becomes happier. She discovers reasons to smile, when she smiles.

# # #

Sid tells the story about arriving at the garage to pick up his car. It was suppose to be ready at 2:00 PM. He arrived at 2:15 PM only to discover that they had not yet looked at his car. Sid spoke to the manager.

"This is a problem for me. I am very busy today. The reason that I set up the appointment was that I did not have the time to wait while you repaired the car. I'm not angry, but I must tell you that I will take the car somewhere else if you cannot fix it right now.

"I will have the next available mechanic work on your car, as soon as he is free," the manager said.

Moments later a grumbling and irritated mechanic stumbled into the room, muttering, "Which one is next?"

Sid took one look at that mechanic and said to the manager, "I would rather wait."

The manager looked puzzled. "Wasn't this the guy who was in such a hurry?"

Sid noticed the manager's consternation. He felt compelled to reply. "Have you ever screwed up a delicate project when you were having a good day? Is it worse when you are having a bad day? This guy is not in a mood that will heal my car."

He was right, of course. Stress hampers patience, manual dexterity, and even our thought process.

# # #

In a psychological experiment, patients were asked to choose between two physicians, as the best doctor for them. The two "physicians" were really actors playing the role of "doctor". One played the part of a senior, exceptionally skilled surgeon, with a bad attitude. The other played a "green" medical student with little experience but a pleasant attitude. When asked which surgeon they would prefer to do their operation, the patients, almost universally, selected the medical student with the poor experience, but the great attitude.

As customers, even of highly technical services, we prefer to be 'served" by people with a great attitude.

# # #

When Sid's own father was scheduled for sensitive cardiac surgery, his family doctor recommended a highly competent doctor who happened to be pessimistic and grumpy. Sid and his family made the decision to turn down assistance from that doctor and went instead to a hospital three hours away, where they found a doctor who was both competent and cheerful.

When Sid was waiting for his father to come out of surgery, in that busy Houston hospital, he was seated in a position to watch the surgeons walk down the hall to the waiting room. Sometimes the surgeons would be smiling. Sometimes they would not. As a family member of someone in surgery, he was praying for a smiling surgeon. By the time Sid's father came out of surgery, it was late afternoon. Many of the surgeons had been on their feet, in a stressful, life or death situation, since six o'clock in the morning. As they broke through the double doors at the end of the corridor, many of their faces were strained and weary. Most of them, certainly the kind ones, remembered where they were going, and who they were going to see, part way down the corridor. They applied a smile and strode up to the patient's family, confidently. A smile is a way that we display confidence, competence and optimism.

Weary as they were, those brave men and women, adjusted their attitude to meet the needs of their patients' families. The smile on Sid's dad surgeon said all that needed to be said about the success of the operation. Everything he said about the operation was just a bonus. The smile was the key that turned the lock for the family. It was all they needed to "hear".

# # #

One time, Sid was hired to help a restaurant deal with its customer service. Sid watched the operation for a short time and approached the owner. Sid said, "The restaurant does a pretty good job with customer service all except for Mary. That woman is the meanest woman I have ever met."

"Oh, Mary, once you get to know her, you'll love her," the owner said, reassuring Sid.

"You really like her, don't you?" Sid asked the owner.. "You would like to see her continue to get pay checks and do well personally?"

"Sure, she's great!" the owner said.

"You'd be wise to pay her to stay home, then. That way she would be happy, and well paid, and your customer service would improve dramatically," Sid added.

"Oh, you just need to get close to her," the owner stated.

"How do you pet a rattlesnake?" Sid asked.

# # #

Smiling triggers an attitude adjustment and sends a message about the attitude about the "smiler" to the customer, which is critical.

# # #

Some of the things Sid is asked to do, as a consultant, are a bit unusual.   One of the most interesting was for a company, growing rapidly, that needed to open a new division. They asked Sid to help them hire a new cohort of employees based on the applicant's potential to give world class customer service.

Sid was placed in an office at the company and interviews were scheduled. Sid asked each applicant a series of questions.   One was, "Do you smile a lot?"

One particularly sour looking man looked grimly straight at Sid and said, in response to that question, "I am known as a smiler."

"Perhaps you better tell your face," Sid thought to himself. Every single applicant had told him that they smile all the time. Almost no one smiled while they told him. There were few smiles in the rest of the interview, with that man, or most of the other people interviewed. Have any of the readers been smiled at too much today?   Have people smiles been just too annoying to you today? Are you surrounded by too many happy people?

Sid gained two insights:

(1) Almost everyone thinks they smile all the time

and

(2) Very few people smile all the time.

Most of the people reading this book believe they are very generous with their smiles. But, the reader should ask themselves about their friends and family: how many of their friends actually do smile most of the time. The sheer probability is that the reader, like the people Sid interviewed, probably doesn't smile as much as he/she thinks (s)he does.

Should you smile even when you don't feel like it? Absolutely! We have a choice, you see, we can smile and become one of those pleasant people that everyone enjoys being with ... or not. We can smile and become healthier and live longer... or not. We can live a life full of more happiness and fun by choosing to smile and be cheerful... or we can choose to be miserable. It won't happen if we don't work at it.

Attitude, happiness, smiling is a choice. It is a choice critical to our health, the happiness of our family and friends, and our business success. Grumpy people are not viewed as people who give good customer service. They are not seen as competent, they get lower employee evaluations, and they are less productive. Further, their lives are shorter.

# # #

T — Tone of Voice

The second step in Sid's steps program for front line customer service representatives is *tone of voice*.

People establish their first impression about you in seven seconds. When people first meet you in those first seven seconds, they don't hear what you say. They hear how you say it. Research on job interviews, indicates that often the decision is made in the first few minutes.

The next time you are with a dog try this: Say, "Come here you nasty animal. I am going to beat you within an inch of your life." But, do it with a cooing, loving, warm tone. The dog will come immediately to your side, tail wagging, eagerly anticipating the encounter. At a later point, call the dog, using these words, "Come hear you sweet heart. Come to papa (or mama). Come here, you darling." Only, this time, do it through clenched teeth. Use a really mean tone. Be nasty. The dog will probably slink away.

Our tone probably communicates more than our words. Why is it when we watch a couple in that fresh bloom of new love that one of them cresses the face of the other, looks deeply to his or her eyes and murmurs softly, but affectionately , "I love you."

Years later it is reduced to a passing and off-handed, "Love ya." The reply appears to be "UNGHH" What does that mean, "UNGHH", a muttered utterance with no form or substance?

We wonder whether anybody reading this has had someone tell them that they love them, too much today. Did they do it too sincerely? Did they look into your eyes too deeply? Were their soft tender cresses too intrusive in your life today?

You see, sometimes, we keep the words of support and caring, but we lose the tone of voice and the facial expression. And, the substance of the interaction disappears. Then people ask, "What's wrong with this relationship?"

In romance, tone of voice is often the first casualty. Its loss will precipitate plenty of other losses.

Focusing on the tone of voice that we use with customers will do a great deal toward resolving conflicts and developing customer relationships.

One teenager attended one of Sid's seminars, and at this point in the seminar, he turned to his mother and said, "So that's what you mean about me having a bad attitude." As a school superintendent for 20 plus years, Fran believes that if adolescents could follow these steps, parental problems with teenagers would be reduced by 50 percent.

E — Expression/Facial

This is very important. As you read the book, take a minute to find your happy and excited expression. Apply it to your face. Now try to say, with the happy and excited expression on your face, "You really piss me off. Or... You really make me mad. Or... You are fired." As you can see, it is not easy to do and it never comes across as authentic, when you do this with a smile.

Fran sometimes sits looking at the audience when Sid presents. Sid has a magical face. He takes more risks with his facial expressions than any other person Fran ever saw.

So, Sid is in the middle of one of these stories. His eyebrows are raised high. His eyes are wide, and, his mouth is all contorted to one side. Guess what Fran sees in the face of the people sitting in the audience... You got it! Their eye brows are raised. Their eyes are wide and their mouth is contorted to one side. When you have a pleasant expression on your face, your customers will too.

Imitating the other person's facial expression is the first thing we all learn as infants. We never unlearn it. Try it.

There are two lessons in this observation about facial expressions.

1. Facial expressions really do affect your customers.

2. Take a risk with your face. Be expressive, particularly about empathy, support, caring, and optimism.

One time Sid was flying home from a seminar when he opened a conversation with the woman sitting next to him.

She indicated that she was just returning from a seminar. Sid asked what kind of seminar.

"It was a seminar about polygraph testing," she answered.

"How do <u>you</u> use lie detector tests?" Sid asked.

"I am a State Trooper," she stated matter-of-factly.

Sid had to admit his surprise, but asked, "I've heard that people can trick a lie detector test merely by changing their expression on their face."

"Yes," the trooper said, observing Sid closely, "it takes a lot of work   Most people can't do that, but I suspect you could."

Lie detector tests use multiple physiological measures to identify stress. Most people, when telling a lie, while they are being observed, will have increased stress. It will show up immediately in increased perspiration and increased blood pressure, and the multiple needles will jump. It is amazing that by manipulating facial expressions, some people can even manipulate the amount of stress their body feels, enough to fool a sophisticated test, like the polygraph.

I wonder if any one who will ever read this book will indicate that they have just the right amount of stress, or will they all feel as virtually everyone does in the seminars that they have too much stress?

The behavior of people at seminars is an indicator of stress levels. People raise their hand timidly in response to a question, for fear of providing a wrong answer. They stand in the back of the room, in hopes of not being noticed. We all bear far too much stress.

The good news is that by changing our facial expression we can minimize the impact of that stress on our bodies.

The best reason to give good customer service is that it works for us. A pleasant, warm, engaging facial expression impacts our customers the same way that the smile on the face of the surgeon impacts the families in the waiting room. And.....it lowers our stress.

# # #

P — Posture or body language

Body language gives us away. Tight folded arms across one's chest, while tilted back in a chair, reveals skepticism

"Oh, Yeah?" screams the body of a person in that position.

If they are smiling, with a pleasant facial expression, there is a disconnect between their face and their body. It turns out we all read body language pretty easily. Most of us can't articulate exactly what we see, that let's know the meaning of someone's posture. But let me give you a simple quiz.

1. A boy is shuffling toward you. His head is bent forward and turned slightly to the left. His shoulders are stooped forward as well. His arms are hanging loosely from their sockets. He does not walk directly toward you but slightly to your left, just a foot or so away. He is looking at the ground. If there were a freshly broken lamp on the other side of the room, would you guess that the boy was about to confess to the accident?

2. A young woman leans forward in her chair and looks directly into a young man's eyes at a restaurant, lips slightly parted. Her pupils are dilated. Her elbows are resting on the table ahead of her cradling her chin. Would you guess that she had a romantic interest in the young man across the table?

3. A man leans forward in his chair. His arms are on the table in front of him. One elbow is resting on the table with that forearm slightly elevated. The

knuckles of that hand are the highest point on that knuckle of that arm. His lips are resting gently on that knuckle and his eyes are cast softly downward. If you had just asked a tough question, would you think that he was taking that question pretty seriously and giving it some thought?

4.   You observe a woman in a grocery store speaking to a young man. She is leaning forward. Her hand gesture is strong. Her thumb touches her index and middle finger. The last two fingers of her hand are pulled tight against her palm. Her hand is high near her mouth. The index and middle finger have their backs to the mouth of the man in front of her. Her thumb is pointing right at his mouth. The hand keeps bobbing up and down rhythmically as she speaks. She stands comfortably erect. Her shoulders are square. If you were standing at some distance to her, would you guess that she is trying to make a particular point of emphasis?

If you answered yes to the four questions above, you are pretty typical. Most of us read body language pretty well. Sid argues that we read body language better than we listen. He may be right.

No one can say for sure, but we probably communicated with body language for millions of years before our species invented speech. Our understanding of body language is probably instinctive. It certainly can be a tool that we can use to communicate with our customers.

How may I help you? with an angry customer, or even in a neutral moment, or perhaps in a happy moment, Sid's body language remains pretty constant. Sid is quick to look people squarely in the eye, thrust out his right hand, and say "Hi. I am Sid Hurlbert. May I help you?" Few of us are disciplined enough or mean enough to refuse to shake hands. Once you shake hands and look somebody in the eye, it is hard to be mean. Sid tries to make every encounter personal, fun, and engaging. He makes his body do, around strangers, what it does around family and friends. Sid alert to signs of resistance or uncomfortableness, but he is quick to put his arm on the shoulder of someone he is talking to, in a gesture that displays sympathy and friendship.

People-watching can be a great sport, if you take it seriously. Fran works at a college. People walk at colleges. The buildings are often close together, parking is often a problem. So, all kinds of people walk together: students and students, students and faculty, faculty and faculty, faculty and deans, deans and students, presidents and students... Here is an interesting observation. People, who like each other, while walking together, eventually will get their steps in the same rhythm. Boyfriends and girlfriends holding hands put the right foot forward at the same time and then the left. The lanky, long limbed basketball player will stutter step to stay in synch with the short perky gymnast.

They don't do this on purpose. They just do it.

Fran always sits by the window in the dining hall. He watches people walk. Faculty with faculty, faculty with deans ... He can always tell the campus politics by watching them walk. People reveal themselves through their rhythms.

People whose feet are badly out of step rarely agree in their words or ideas. Rhythms are important.

The highest form of flattery is imitation. In fact, our civilization depends on people imitating, instinctively, those people that they like and love. Why do babies imitate their parents? Why do we hope, or sometimes fear, students will imitate teachers? We are driven to do it. Intuitively we know someone likes us when they imitate us. We know, without noticing why, that someone likes us when they walk in synch.

It is, curiously, that much like the body language above, we all know what this means. We begin to notice that we have a friend, or a lover, or a confident. We cannot analyze why. The body language is communicating. We read it, we understand it, we make decisions and commitments based on it, yet, it all happens beyond our understanding.

How can we use this information to help us work with others? The answer, in part, is about rhythms and synchronicity.

A customer comes into complain. We, of course, thrust out our hand. "Hi, I am Sid. How can I help you?" The customer stands, feet, shoulder wide, arms tightly folded, leaning forward. (This is a classic aggressive posture, slightly defensive.)

We have a choice. We can either assume his position, indicating we understand him, and gently imitate every change in posture indicating we like him and agree with him, or we can initiate a softer and gentler body language, warm, expressive, and open, guiding him, and inviting him to see our body language, and imitate it, and thereby change his fundamental psychological orientation.

The first option of pure imitation is pretty easy to do. Even those of us who don't have much formal knowledge about body language, can simply take the cues from our customers and move with them, from aggressive to a more relaxed body language.

This approach will work, most of the time. However, imitating an aggressive body language may cause the customer to become more aggressive. So, Sid takes a different approach. Sid begins with the out stretched hand, "Hi, I am Sid. How may I help?"

This moves the person out of the most aggressive body language. Sid listens to the initial outburst, and then says, "Follow me." Sid walks to any other location in the store or office. The person follows Sid, usually to a counter or a desk. Sid puts the counter between himself and the person. The person has to imitate Sid to get there. The customer follows Sid's rhythms. All of the body language has changed. Now Sid, "protected", by the counter, can safely imitate the body language of the person on the other side of the counter, indicating, subconsciously, that he has empathy for the person's problem and is in touch with the person's emotions.

This method works. (Most of the time)

The alternative is to learn about body language and train your body to respond in a way that diffuses tense situations and makes people comfortable. Actors study body language. They learn how to use their body deceptively and communicate to others, powerful messages that they may, in fact, not be feeling. It takes years of practice for most people. Shortcuts here are hard to come by. But here is a technique that may help.

One technique to learn how to use your body to communicate warmth, empathy and caring is to "Freeze frame" moments when you are with people you like doing things that you like to do. Stop. Notice the way you are sitting, standing, and leaning. Learn how that feels. Reproduce it at time when you need to show other people that you are happy, comfortable, and acting in their best interest.

Then roll it out in a tense or not so tense situation so that others will see your body language and understand that you are a friend working in their behalf.

At any rate, don't leave your body language to chance.

# # #

Sid went to a presentation about love and kindness by a very powerful scholar. Sid was thinking about how powerful the material was, when he happened to notice that most of the audience was not paying any attention, whatsoever, to the speaker. He wondered why until he noticed the grim countenance of the presenter.

What should the body language and tone be of a person urging you to be kind and loving? His brilliant words were lost due to his frowning face.

# # #

Sid does 200 seminars a year. He is always on the road and he has more experience than the average preacher speaking to crowds.

It is a funny thing to speak at seminars. Everywhere you go, there are certain commonalities. Preachers observe the same things. The back seats fill first. When you ask a question, no one raises their hand. When and if the hands do go up, they go up timidly. They raise briskly to shoulder height and then just as quickly retreat to the owner's table or lap.

What is that? Why are people like that? Why don't people stride down to the front seats and confidently raise their hands when a question is raised?

# # #

One time, at a seminar at Cornell University, Sid confirmed his suspicions about why people act that way. The audience was milling about in the entry foyer to the auditorium. The last few people were coming in from outside, where some had just extinguished their cigarettes. The crowd had just begun to enter the auditorium. A man was next to Sid as they funneled into that large room.

"Do you have to go to this damn thing, too." The man asked. His face was contorted with barely contained anger.

Yeah," Sid said. "I suppose I do."

"I have so much to do, I could almost spit," the man sputtered. "I don't know why they are dragging me to this thing. This thing is probably just another huge waste of time."

"Probably so," Sid said.

"I am going to protest this one," the man replied. They probably are going to tell us to go sit down front, like they usually do."

"He is right again," Sid thought.

"This time I am going to protest. I am not only not going to sit down front, I am not going to sit at all," the man sputtered.

"Me too," Sid said, "Where are you going to stand?"

"I am going to stand right in the back," the man said. "The jerk that organized this thing won't get it, but, I will feel better. I will feel like I made a statement."

"I agree with you," Sid said. "I am going to stand, too, all the way through this seminar. But, I am going to do you one better. I am going to stand down front."

"Oh, don't do that. You'll really get them mad," the man advised.

"I don't _care_. Something has to be done about this." Sid strode down to the front of the auditorium.

He stood against the wall, his facing glaring out at the audience.

The man standing in the back had a very worried expression and urgently gestured for Sid to join him in the back.

Sid shook his head, "no", defiantly, and held his ground at the side of the front of the auditorium.

The man in the back was worried.

Sid was making a fool of himself.

The man in the back regretted that he had suggested this protest. When Sid was introduced, and took his place at the podium, the man slinked quietly to a seat.

After the presentation, the man approached Sid. "I'm sorry about all that stuff before you started. I really needed this seminar more than I thought I did. Thanks for not embarrassing me by telling what I did."

Sid smiled and gave the big guy a hug.

Body language makes a difference.

In the story above, Sid's body language, when standing against the wall in the front, was a mirror of the body language of the angry man. When he hugged him, he was warm with laughter. Body language helps.

We can smile with, and tease, and cajole, even our difficult customers. The seminar and the interaction with Sid were probably even more meaningful for the reluctant attendee than for the rest.

# # #

S — Start putting into people what you want back.

The last step in Sid's step program is *start putting into people what you want back.*

Can you tell when someone is angry with you when they approach you? Is there something about their body language, facial expression and demeanor that tells you that you are in trouble?

A lot of customer conflict comes from what we bring to the table. We put the stress in the encounter by our behavior. Most of us have had to deal with angry teachers, principals, and even, sadly, angry parents. Encountering those powerful people, angry, early in our lives, we had no real way to develop a mature approach to angry people. Many of us, and many of our customers, have inappropriate reactions to stern, doubtful, or angry faces.

Let's offer a concrete example:

Sid loves to carry a tiny tape recorder. He loves to tape interactions with front line people. He records the best and the worst, and tries to learn from them. Sid bought a micro cassette recorder from a well known national chain, when the recorders first came out. He was pleased that this tiny device would allow him to record these interactions, even more surreptitiously, than he could previously.

It was a new product line. The very first one he received didn't work.. He returned it to the store, to a high school aged employee, working alone at night.

(How many of us hate to bring things back to the store where we bought them, even when we have the receipt and the product doesn't work? We don't like to bring them back. Most of us anticipate some level of conflict.)

When Sid approached this young employee with his problem, the boy's face frowned. He folded his arms and asked, "How did it break?"

Sid knew immediately what the boy really was asking, which was, "What stupid thing did you do, to break it?" Sid persevered, he explained that he simply took it out of the box, installed the batteries, and it did not work.

The boy played with the recorder. He also couldn't get it to work. Somewhat reluctantly, he gave Sid a new one. Sid went home, put in the batteries, and this one, too, did not work. How would you feel returning this second device to the same pimply faced kid the next day? How would you feel asking, this time, for your money back and not simply a replacement for this twice broken device? As you entered the store, what's your facial expression? What is your body language? What is your demeanor?

The innocent high school student is watching, as the door flies open and a freight train bears upon him.

Let's pretend he was coached by Sid, and knew what to do.

"I am really annoyed," the customer might sputter. "This stupid cassette recorder..."

"Hi, I am David Tait," the boy would say, warmly thrusting his hand out to be shaken.

"Hi, I am Sid Hurlbert," Sid would mutter. His intent to be rude already thwarted. The context had just changed. This was no longer about a frustrating cassette recorder. It was now about two people just being introduced. The boy had put into Sid what he wanted out.

Sid would then explain his problems with the cassette recorder and the history of this purchase. The boy (trained by Sid, remember) would say to Sid, "Follow me, sir."

(Mermer Blakeslee, author of the book, In the Yikes! Zone, a book about fear and negative emotions, talks about getting people out of fearful places by getting them to follow simple directions and moving them through simple rhythmical movements.)

Sid finds that asking customers to follow him takes the pressure out of the situation. He moves them to a second counter. They have now followed his direction and are more compliant. He is now ready to solve their situation. The person in the customer service roll has also had time to think.

When you put into other people what you want back, you can change other peoples' behavior. When Sid first started consulting, he got a lot of mail from his customers. He got so much mail that the only practical solution for mail delivery was to open a post office box. Sid did not like to go to that post office to pick up his mail. They were mean. Sid had to go there to get his mail, but he didn't like it.

Sid decided to put into them what he wanted back. He smiled. He used a lot of inviting facial expression. He told stories. He engaged them personally. He expressed an interest in them. It soon became less of "us" and "them" situation and more of a "we" situation, as they began to laugh together, frequently. One day Sid turned the combination lock on his mail box. He opened the door. He put his hand in to retrieve his mail and as he did, a hand inside the mail box grabbed his. He nearly had a heart attack. When he retrieved his arm, he looked through the opening in the mail box, nothing could be seen but, he heard peels of laughter coming from the area behind the mail boxes. He went to the customer service window and looked behind the mailboxes, where one person, who had originally been a particular old sourpuss, was laughing so hard that he was laughing and crying at the same time.

The breakthrough was complete. Sid had put into the post office employees what he wanted back, and he no longer dreaded getting the mail. By controlling his own attitude and putting into them what he wanted back, Sid changed the way they behaved toward him. Can't we do this with our customers? Can't we take them on as projects, one at a time?

Once at the second counter, the high school aged clerk can do what has to be done. Two of these recorders have failed. Cheerfully return the money and express sincere regret. What else can you do? Lets just do it stylishly.

#

Don't you think most of your customers want to be treated respectfully? Wouldn't they like their encounters with you to be human? Couldn't this approach work for you?

#

Will this approach work for everyone?

No.

Some won't try it.

There is an aspect of following this approach that makes one feel like a performer. "You mean that I have to be outgoing? You mean I have to greet my customer, shake hands, and introduce myself? You mean I have to smile at my customers and try to engage them?"
Not if you want long days, miserable customers and a failing business. If that is what you want, don't try these techniques. These techniques will have just the opposite effect.

Some people won't want to try this approach out of fear. They won't have the confidence. They will have no self-esteem or low self esteem. They will fear rejection. They will be concerned that they are too young, too old, too well dressed, or not dressed well enough. They will fear that they are too fat. They will be concerned about what will happen if the customer learns about their education or lack of it, their car, their house, or their neighborhood. "Suppose they meet my family?"

"I met your brother the other day," someone said.

"He is not my brother. He just says he is. Nope, not him, not that loud hairy guy."

# # #

A two year old could walk across a stage, buck naked peeing as he walked. He would smile, delighted to be watching the people watching him. He would not be self conscious. He would remain confident and, at ease.

Things happen to us between when we were two years old, and now. And, not all of it was good. A drop in confidence may have been one of the things we lost that we shouldn't have.

# # #

Kids, unaffected by our adult fears, can work us like a lion tamer works his lions.

All parents give kids the same instructions when they enter a store. "Don't touch anything. Don't ask for anything."

We watch them in the stores. The other day we watched a cute little four year old girl pick up toy after toy in the discount store. She begged. We were too far away to hear the father but we could see his lips say no. As she brought each item to his attention, she dropped a shoulder and got a sincere and pleading look on her face.

I was prepared to shove him out of the way, and buy the toys for her myself.

She managed to put one of the toys in his hands and when he picked it up, she applied a very hopeful smile on her face. I was sure he would tumble this time. He put it in the cart. She won again. She rewarded him with a face splitting smile.

Here is the critical question. Did that four year old girl go out to the car and read a book on how to handle rejection and how to get what she wants?

No.

We all start out being pretty good at this, and get worse, as we believe the negative things that people tell us about ourselves.

Sid is an interesting case in point. He was a pretty good student in Penn Yan High School, but college was not in his future. College was simply not a part of his family's experience. No one had planned for the college tuition costs. His counselors and teachers did not urge him to go to college, in spite of his good grades. He didn't come from a college oriented family. In those days that may have been a more important cause of success than academic laurels.

When he finished high school, like so many other kids of his socio-economic class, started some businesses and worked at others, where his extraordinary ability to work well with customers became celebrated. In time, Sid was making presentations across the country. Large and small universities brought him to speak, frequently. He lived in terror, however, of being asked "What college did you go to?"

We all seem to have reasons to hide rather than shine. Sid is not going to change his educational background. He is running seminars 200 days a year. He does not have the time or the inclination to go back to school, now. There are things about all of us that cause us to retreat into ourselves instead of coming forward confidently.

Often these reasons are old, foolish ones, like Sid's concern about not having gone to college. Hell, now Sid trains college professors.

# # #

One time Sid was the second speaker on a program. The first speaker was handsome, slender and well dressed. Sid is anything but slender. The first speaker's high level of education oozed out through his language. Sid is plain spoken. Sid watched the man on the stage and, for one of the first times in his life, he thought, 'I don't really want to go on. I don't want to follow him."

There are days like that for all of us. Sid forced himself onto the stage. He reached out to shake hands with the first speaker as they passed walking across the stage. The first speaker ignored his outstretched hand. The speaker had refused to shake his hand. Sid pulled back his arm and kept going. He was sure everyone there saw that snub.

Sid, now, really didn't want to be there, speaking. But, he dug deep. He smiled. He put into his audience what he wanted back. He modulated his tone of voice and brought a warm empathic facial expression to his presentation. The handsome young speaker saw him after the presentation and asked Sid to share with him how he works with an audience like that.

The other speaker wanted to achieve what Sid had.

Sweet revenge.

# # #

Confidence is crucial

We would all be more effective if we followed Sid's STEPS, but, we have to recapture the confidence we had in pre-school in order to be as effective as we need to be.

Sid had an experience with an airline that really put a fine point on this. The story is a common one, as it begins. An airplane skidded off the runway in Chicago. Many flights to and from Chicago were cancelled including Sid's. He, and a lot of other people, were stuck in San Antonio waiting to get to Chicago. Sid kept his optimism. He controlled his tone of voice and his facial expressions. He smiled at the airline representative. He put into her what he wanted back. He teased her, played with her, and engaged her warmly. He explained that he was due to present the next day in Chicago, a seminar for 240 people. There was no alternate date.

The airline representative began typing furiously searching for a ticket for Sid. She put together a flight that took two stops to get Sid to Kenosha, Wisconsin. Sid would rent a car from there and make it to Chicago on time.

Sid was pleased.

Sid asked the woman, "Were these flights full?"

"No, they are practically empty," she replied.

"What about these other people?" Sid inquired.

"I guess they will have to cool their heels," she replied. "Sometimes people get what they deserve, especially when their attitude is poor. I don't owe these people anything. You, you're different."

# # #

The STEPS Sid shares with audiences across the United States are all pretty basic. Most of us know that if we consistently employ these STEPS, we would be more effective with our customers.

Unfortunately, familiarity breeds comfort. There is no personal risk in continuing to do what we have always done. There is, however, little chance that we will improve our relationships with others, by staying the same.   Not changing brings no risk of embarrassment, but it insures a risk of not improving, above where we are now.

Most of us will be trapped in San Antonio, as "we deserve".   Some of us will take some personal risks and be routed to Kenosha. From there, with initiative, we could drive to Chicago.   Those of us who do, will get to where we want to go, when we want to get there, and succeed.

# # #

Celebrate people

Earlier we talked about the power of habit. We can become captives of our own habits. Sometimes that is a good thing. Bathing works pretty well. Sid and Fran are pleased to report that each of us has a habit of bathing. It makes it easier when we get together.

Habit takes a funny hold on us, however. There was a report not long ago that men each shave their face the same way every time.   Sid starts on the upper right on his face, works toward his chin, and …He tried to start on the left and nearly required a transfusion from the loss of blood that resulted from the razor nicks. The whole skill-set of shaving was based on a series of sub-routines that were conducted in a particular order. Changing the order required the skill set to be rebuilt.

Habit is not always a bad thing. Habit is why Major League Baseball players can hit the ball with some consistency. It is why good golfers have a pattern of success.

Wouldn't it be awful if every time we reached for a cup of coffee on the table we had to solve the problem of how to take a sip all over again each time? Much of our life is spent in repetition. Our habits in the morning, from moment we turn off the alarm clock, until we arrive at the office are pretty routine. Our habits help us to get through this time period efficiently, even while half awake.

Not all habits, however, are helpful – especially those that belittle other people.

Most of us are unaware of these habits, unless other people bring them to our attention. Even then, we tend to reject them. ("My boss told me I am sometimes abrupt...That idiot, what does he know?") It is hard to hear this kind of criticism. We all think we are pretty good with people. If you look around you, however, you'll realize that someone who is truly gifted with people is unusual, indeed. Objectively, we cannot all be great with people. Probably, if you are like Sid and I, you could stand some improvements in this area. Who couldn't?

The habits we have that are not great, in our dealings with people, we probably did not select. Children are like sponges for new information and behaviors. As we get older, our ability to learn some things declines. (There is pretty good research, for example, that very few people can learn a foreign language without an accent after the age of 12. The researchers believe that vocal muscles cannot be trained to go outside a certain range after that age.)

So, while we are being human sponges, powerful adults in our environment show us how to treat others, for example, when we are disappointed. Those role models are parents, teachers, scout leaders, coaches, principals, and others who dealt with us when we disappointed them.

So, Joyce who works with Sid and Fran comes into the office a little frazzled from difficult deadlines and complex tasks. Fran says to Joyce, "Did you get that letter out to Ralph?"

"Oh darn, I forgot." Joyce might reply.

The most important thing Fran will do will happen in the next millisecond. Sid likes to say that you feel 30 times faster than you act and you act 30 times faster than you think.

Most of us are going to act before we think about it based on a feeling of disappointment which will cause our blood pressure to rise. As a species, normally we approach this moment as a "ready, fire, aim" situation rather than a "ready, aim, fire" situation. Our behavior is so fast it feels like we don't have any control over it. Do you ever regret those moments when you fire from the lip?

What we actually do, at that moment, is to play the old tapes from childhood. We might roll our eyes. We might shake our head no. We might say, "tsk, tsk, tsk." We might explode in pointless rage.

There are, of course, better options.

Joyce is a remarkable person. In her heart, she wants Sid and Fran to succeed more than they do. She gets it right 95 percent of the time. Ninety-five percent got her pretty good grades in high school, college, and graduate school. Her accuracy and follow through made her a successful teacher and school administrator.

What should the response to Joyce be? How could Fran respond, leaving her ego intact? How could Fran communicate to her about this, and let her know that she is a valued member of the team, a friend, and a person that he cares about?

How about, "Pobody is nerfect?" Because, nobody is perfect.

We should never let go of our task orientation. If the work is not important, perhaps we should be doing something else. It is not appropriate to abandon the commitment to the task. But, if we abuse the members of the team because of our blind commitment to the task, we will be locked in a downward spiral. We need to look at our habits in dealing with people and to adopt new behaviors that celebrate the people in our lives.

# # #

Handling mistakes

Mistakes are inevitable. Fran often talks about how he has about a five percent error rate. About five percent of the time, no matter what he his doing, he will make a mistake. Five percent of the time when he leaves his driveway, he turns the wrong way. Five percent of time when he goes to the grocery store he brings home the wrong item or forgets something. These mistakes cut across the big issues, too. Five percent of the time as a school superintendent, he screwed up a conversation with a taxpayer, a citizen, or a parent. Most of the time, these mistakes are not critical. When turning the wrong way coming out of the driveway, you turn around and come back. They are not very costly because, frankly, most of what Fran does, in life, is not a life or death decision.

Are any of us dramatically different from this? Do we have a two percent error rate or a three percent error rate? Even so, it is an error rate. Error is a constant. It may be impossible to remove it from any human system.

Yet, in spite of the fact that we all make mistakes, sometimes we handle the other person who made the mistake, the way people handled us when we made mistakes as children. "How could you be so stupid?" Or, "Did you leave your brain at home?"

Our brains are pretty imperfect computers. It is easier to engineer a computer chip to make no errors than an organ with blood vessels, cholesterol, and a high reliance of oxygen and micronutrients. Some error would be expected by the nature of the design of the organ called the brain. After all, even some of those computer chips sometimes make mistakes.

Now, let's confuse the organ with not enough sleep or exercise.

Why do we jump all over somebody who made a mistake? The mistake has already been made. Generally speaking, there is little the person can do to unmake it. The work should go into helping them not make the mistake in the first place by defining the task better and "dip-sticking" their performance early on all the sub-tasks that lead to the eventual success or failure of their work on the larger mission.

When a person comes to you to say, "I made a mistake", they, of course, know they made a mistake. That is often how you found out about it in the first place. Most people feel very badly about mistakes especially the serious ones that hurt others. They don't generally need to be reminded of that, or berated.

Sid had a four hour seminar at a company that had made attendance mandatory for a group of employees. The group was mostly assembled. Sid moved forward to the microphone. He smiled at the group in anticipation of launching his presentation. Just as he was about to begin, a woman charged into the back of the room. Sid observed her, still in her coat, carrying her briefcase. She looked at him and gave an exasperated sigh.

Not all of Sid's thoughts at this moment were happy ones. He thought "this is going to be a tough group." He thought "I am sorry she made it."

He said, however, kindly, "We've not yet begun. Why don't you hang up your coat, get yourself a cup of coffee, and I will begin in a few minutes." She glared at him, still, as if he were the one being rude, and then, hung up her coat and got coffee.

Sid is a very effective presenter, and a lot of what he shares touches people's hearts. In an audience of all women, some of the points he makes will cause tears. In an audience of all men, when Sid reaches a similar point in his presentations, there will be a lot of throat clearing. The woman who was late got to such a point in his presentation, where he was talking about the need for parents to treat their children with dignity. She began to fall into shoulder shaking sobs.

When the presentation was all over, she approached Sid, as the other employees were exiting the room. She explained to Sid that earlier, that very morning her husband announced that he was leaving her. He was moving in with another woman. He was filing papers for a divorce. He provided her a date when he, and the movers, would come to pick up his stuff. As her husband left the house, after this bomb shell, their 11 year old daughter looked her mother straight in the eye and said, "It's my fault, isn't mommy?"

"I dropped her off at school, trying to explain cheerfully, what I had experienced tearfully." She threw her arms around Sid's shoulders. "Thank you so much," she said. "I really needed this seminar more than I knew. Today I learned my husband of 15 years is divorcing me. My daughter thinks it is her fault. I was running late and feeling terrible. When I came into the room, I thought that you were going to attack me because I was late. Instead, you were nice to me, and what you had to say helped me very much."

We cannot know all that goes on behind the eyes of the person looking at us. Most of us have too many examples of how to use ill considered reprimand, sarcasm, or even an "off-handed" gesture, to put us in our place. We need to find better alternatives than the examples provided to us.

Would we be better or nobler and more effective, if we respond instead with empathy, while still insisting that we all work to improve the system for our customers?

# # #

Sid also likes to urge people to smile in a difficult confrontation. Sid always says that a smile reveals confidence, competence, and strength.   But, one reason he offers for the smile, comes from this question. Who do you have more to fear from, in a confrontation, a person who is swearing at you and calling you names, or a person who has a broad grin?

Wouldn't you wonder why that person is smiling?

PART

II

## CHAPTER 3

Reframing

The S.T.E.P.S. program and all that comes easier, in this book, can be very helpful to people engaged in customer service. However, even a close following of those principles won't allow the reader to duplicate all of Sid's and Fran's amazing success with people. Sid and Fran offer a second seminar, for an even a deeper look. The substance of which is captured in this section of this book.   It focuses on the idea of "reframing".

Reframing is a simple idea, but hard to do. That is why Sid doesn't introduce it, except by example, in his introductory seminars.   It only works if people use it with a twinkle in their eye. Sometimes it doesn't work at all. We can use it to adjust our own behavior or we can use it with others, individually or in groups. More on that, later.

Often, much more often than we would like to admit, everyone's thinking gets stuck. At these times, we, too often, see the world with blinders on. Let us provide you with an example.

Although there is some debate about the actual facts about the way European sailors saw the world prior to 1492, most of us understand that European sailboats stayed pretty close the continent, in part, for some, due to a fear of falling off the edge of a flat world. Others simply were afraid of the size of the sea or afraid they would not find their way back.   It took Columbus' insight and his brave act of sailing to the "new" world, to reframe our vision of the world, to see it as a continuous sphere. Reframing is the act of suddenly putting the world in a new context and causing people to see it in a new frame.   Once that happened, the behavior of European sailors was dramatically and permanently altered. That's an example of reframing.

We all hear the dictum, "Think outside the box". One of the disciplines of thinking outside the box is to continuously reframe. People who fail to reframe miss opportunities because their vision is limited. The railroad ran into difficulty, not because of the airplane. They ran into difficulty because they didn't see their business as the transportation business. Transportation incorporates all forms of travel, which could include, potentially, even air travel and air cargo. If they had, Sid's next business trip might be booked on Flight 600 on the Santa Fe and Topeka airlines.

Sid reframes people, places, and events all the time. A waitress grumpily approached him one time demanding, in a surly voice, "What do you want"?

His reply was, "I'll have a new waitress, please."

His reply reframed for that waitress, and that restaurant, the standard of customer service.

An old habit of thinking of the waitress was challenged with an unexpected reply. Her old habit was, "I am an order taker. I don't like doing this, but they pay me. I will do it, but I don't have to be happy about it." Sid's reply caused her to reframe her behavior. It was, for her, the equivalent of Columbus discovering America.

As we will discover later in this section of the book, this act of reframing could not have been done effectively by someone whose demeanor was sarcastic or belittling. It needed to be done by someone who, like Sid, had a twinkle in his or her eye.

The waitress was startled at the reply from Sid. But, she saw he was serious. Reluctantly, she left. Sid got a new waitress. He teased and joked with the new one during his week long stay in that town.

He would sometimes begin the day by giving her a big tip, then explaining he wanted her to see the tip first so she would know the kind of service he expected.

Toward the end of the week, the grumpy waitress asked Sid if she could try again. Her attitude and service was great. During the next few days, she continued to serve Sid well. On Friday, the owner of the restaurant told Sid, "I am going to hate to see you leave." But, Sid could leave. His job was done.

# # #

Change has enemies. Sometimes it seems the whole world is aligned against change. Our own defensiveness is one of the most prominent enemies of personal change. Defenses were a good thing for our species, historically. When our enemies were walking across the African Veldt, our defenses were what kept us alive. Facing a physical threat, our automatic response was "fight or flight". Facing one small lion, armed with a sharp spear, we might fight. Facing a pack of lions, we might exercise our option for flight and run. Those responses, fight or flight, still help us in a complex, and sometimes threatening contemporary environment. Who, reading this book, has not said, "I'm not paying for this. This is ridiculous. You have to take it back." Is this the comtempory instinct to fight?

Who, reading this book, has not hastened her pace back to her car upon hearing footsteps behind her? Is this the same instinct, "wired-in" two million, or more, years ago for flight?

These are contemporary examples of fight or flight.

Defenses can be good. They protect us. When the species acquired speech, it gave our species a new set of defense options. We have all kinds of new ways to defend ourselves in this new "post language" era. We use sarcasm and ridicule. We deny accusations. Sometimes, we lie, even to ourselves. (It is hard to imagine being animals without self deception.) We counter attack. We project our inadequacies and attitudes into others. We blame others for our faults. This is just a beginner's introduction to the sophisticated defenses we use in the 21st Century. Defenses are good, you see, *except when they stop us from seeing ourselves clearly which can stop us from moving ahead.*

As a species, we used to use defenses to defend our lives. Now, we use them to defend our egos. Language made defending ourselves that much easier. Some would argue these "post language" defenses made that "ego defense" way too easy... to our detriment.

Earlier in the book, Sid asked the question, "Who doesn't give good customer service?" When he asks that question in a group, even in a large group, no hands go up. We all think we give good customer service. It is easy for us to see when someone else does not give good customer service to us, but our defenses don't let us see when we don't. The person we all identify as giving lousy customer service probably also has great defenses. There are reasons for his or her behavior. (S)he can't change. (S)he is blind to his/her faults. His/her defenses make him/her blind.

"Are you kind?" we ask, rhetorically.

Are you? Earlier we used the image of Columbus discovering a new world. On the early maps, soon after his discovery, map makers labeled the new world now known as North and South America as "Terra Incognito" (the unknown land). For each of us today, the "Terra Incognito" is too often, ourselves. Are you kind? Do you really know?

Try this simple test of our self-knowledge. Are you good looking? Do you know? Do you really know? Few of us do.

We literally see others more clearly than we see ourselves. We don't bring as much baggage to the appearance of others, especially if we don't know them. But, to ourselves, we do. Recent research reveals that most women see themselves as fatter and less pretty than men see them. Men see themselves as less muscular and less athletic than women see them.

If we could sit at a table with nine other people and anonymously rank them by our impression of their looks from 1-10, as trivial an act as that might be, there would be a remarkable consistency in our evaluation of their looks, for all of them from all observers.   But, we would show a remarkable failure in accurately evaluating our own looks, when compared to the evaluation of the other nine raters.

Who do we see more than anyone else? We (both Sid and Fran) look at ourselves in the mirror every day to shave and several times a day to wash our face, adjust our hair, and....

Why don't we know how we look, when everyone else clearly does? Our ego defenses don't permit us to see ourselves clearly. They are so powerful, they literally cloud our vision of ourselves.

If we are so blind that we can't even accurately see how we look, what other aspects of our lives don't we "see"? Could insight into our strengths improve our performance? Could insights into our weaknesses?   If we could see our assets and liabilities, would it help us be more effective?

The remarkable Scottish poet, Robert Burns, upon observing a beautifully coiffed woman seated ahead of him in church, with a louse crawling up her hair said, "Oh, would some power, the Giftie gie us, to see ourselves as others see us." Translated into contemporary English, it would read, "Oh, would you Lord give us the power to see ourselves as others see us!" The woman was poised in the church pew, basking in her own presumed beauty, not realizing that there were bugs in her hair. But, everyone else could see them.

Psychologists consistently report that peoples' self-rating of their job performance is generally higher than their bosses' rating of their performance. This will come as no surprise to anyone who has had to evaluate personnel.   These are all predictable problems that come from a well-developed set of defenses. That which kept us safe from lions, tigers, and bears (oh my!) interferes, in a highly competitive age, with our ability to assess how well we provide our customers with what they want.

Reframing has the potential to provide short intense sparks of insight.

#

Since the 1960's the psychological literature on change has stated that there are three conditions that have to be met for change to occur:

1.   People and organizations have to have a clear sense of where they want to be. They have to, as Senge states, begin with the end in mind. They have to have, in a customer service perspective, a clear picture of what world class customer service would look like in their organization, before they could do it.

(The first part of this book helps people formulate a vision for themselves.)

2.   People and organizations have to understand where they are now, exactly. This is very hard to do. Defense mechanisms stop us, particularly from seeing our faults.

(Remember, most people think that their customer service is great. But, as customers of multiple companies, we know that is not true always. Should we be worried about our customer service? Reframing can help people gain this insight in a non-threatening way that allows them to hear that insight without becoming defensive. That is one of the reasons we need to know how to reframe situations. We can also use reframing to adjust how customers see our organization, and themselves.)

3. People and organizations have to want to close the gap between where they want to be and where they are now.

(This requires insight and, often, leadership.)

Seen from this perspective, change is not complicated. In fact, if all the above conditions are met, it is hard to stop people and organizations from changing. So, what's the problem? First, people don't see where they are. Second, they often don't have any idea that there is a better way. Therefore, they don't see a gap to close, and therefore, they can't move to close it.

# # #

Why don't we just tell the "mean spirited" waitress in the story above that she has to become engaged more pleasantly with her customers? We'll tell her she is no good the way she is; and, that her customers expect a more considerate approach.

"You are a real nasty waitress. Shape up or ship out", Sid should have told the mean waitress in the restaurant.

Now, there's a good idea.

Not so much.

This would work splendidly, if people didn't have those fight or flight defenses hardwired in. After two million years of success with these defenses, it is hard to throw them overboard. Mark Twain said, "Habit is habit, not to be flung out the window, but to be coaxed down the stairs one step at a time." To confront people directly about their kindness, consideration, or service inadequacies, is to attack them at a very fundamental level of their personality. The possibility of the rejection of your helpful suggestions is very high. This strategy is unlikely to succeed, in most cases. We have all seen it work sometimes, but it fails too frequently to turn to it all the time, as our primary method to solve customer service problems or inadequacies.

# # #

Here is another approach that will fail as easily as the first. Let's provide a lecture to the waitress about good customer service. Let's show her how valuing our customer is important. This approach is designed to give the waitress a clear view of where she needs to go without, addressing the question of where she is now. She may say, indignantly, "Why is he raising these questions with me? Or, she may ask, "What has this got to do with the price of tea in China?"

Worse yet, lets haul in the whole staff to address the problems of one low functioning individual. The whole group will get the lecture, hoping that the one bad apple gets the message. The "good" staff will know who you are trying to address and resent the mandatory lecture. The troubled staff member will still not see this as her problem.

Ask any teacher who is really good at her craft, and she will tell you that teaching is not a group activity. Great teachers engage each student, one at a time, and pile up their successes, one student at a time.

If the reader has attended a seminar by Sid, they will know that other people were in the room, but Sid was really engaging, just them. Sid is a great teacher.

We have all heard the expression, "When the student is ready, the teacher will come". How many lessons have we heard from our parents, teachers, from others, that we were simply not ready to hear? We failed to learn, simply because we were not ready for it.

Were you one of the 90 percent of us who failed to get it when you were told "Don't run up credit card debt?" Do any of us have poor finances because of lack of information about the dangers of indebtedness? Fran always marvels at the problems the public thinks can be solved merely through education. Drug and alcohol education will surely stop abuse of drugs and alcohol. Kids won't use them once they know the risks. No, drugs and alcohol won't recruit new kids just because it is fun to get stoned. And, sex education...

If we don't perceive a need for change, all the sage's advice and lessons given to us, will simply not matter.

Reframing is simply a way in a singular moment to come "up sideways" on one of these problems, not head-on. Coming at it head-on raises defenses. Coming up sideways, in a startling way, allows you to be heard.

Scott Shablak is an extraordinary teacher. When Fran taught with him in a middle school, in Onondaga County, in New York State, there was one particular student who had a problem no one else was able to fix.

"Pete" was a student at that school. There is always one of these boys, like Pete, in every middle school. Maybe you remember the one in your middle school, growing up. He traveled through the hallway, as if he were a car. He made car noises as he moved, and frequently "up shifted" and "downshifted" using his hand on an imaginary shift knob, while adjusting his vocalization. Ask any middle school teacher, and they will identify which student, in his or her school does this, all the time.

These boys, (they are almost always boys) can be pretty geeky. They can be on the edge of autism. They often use their "automobile selves" to keep other people away. The behavior isolates them, happily.

Many teachers had spoken to the boy about the "car" behavior urging him to stop it. They told him kindly that this behavior was inappropriate. They told him that he would have an easier time making friends, if he stopped it. Teachers spoke to his parents. The parents then spoke to Pete about the "problem". He wouldn't give it up.

Intuitively, Scott Shablak understood reframing. Scott asked me to come to his classroom.

"Watch this," he said, as he reached for a small spiral bound assignment pad. He grabbed a pen, and waited by the door to the room, anticipating the sound of our young "automotive boy", Pete. As we heard the sounds of the gearshift up the stairs and along the hall, Scott leaped out the door, with a flourish. He held out an up stretched palm, in a gesture that said, "Halt!" He said dramatically, "Pull over to the curb".

Pete, the "Automotive boy" downshifted to a stop at the edge of the doorway with a startled look on his face. Scott was speaking to him using the very grammar and syntax of his behavior.

Scott dramatically flipped open the assignment pad. He licked the tip of the pencil and held it in position, poised over the pad. "License and registration?" Scott snarled.

The boy looked very uncomfortable and squirmed.

"No license? No registration?" Scott demanded.

The boy looked crestfallen. Scott began to scribble. He said aloud what he was writing, "Unregistered motor vehicle, and unlicensed driver. This is a very serious offense."

The boy began to stammer, as if attempting an explanation.

"I'll let you off easy this time, but if I see you anywhere on this highway again, I am going to impound the vehicle and put you in jail. Leave the car here for now. You can go on, but you are on foot from now on. If your parents want the car, they can come and get it. But for now, it stays here. Got that?"

The boy sheepishly walked away. Curiously, he never "drove" again.

# # #

This was a straightforward case of reframing. Scott put the problem in a different context. He brought the boy's attention to the problem without raising his defenses. He attempted to resolve the problem symbolically. In this case, this symbolic resolution was the resolution. In other situations, reframing brings a clear insight into the problem without truly resolving it. Recovery can require additional steps, and support.

# # #

Reflecting back to the restaurant example from earlier in the book, the waitress was surly. She didn't know she was difficult. Her tone was, "What do you want, Mac?" That's not what Sid wanted. What he wanted was "What can I do to help you this morning, dear?" Sid is pretty good with mornings, but none of us likes our morning to be jarring.

What he said was, "I'll have another waitress."

His request provided him with a different waitress, and as you will remember, from earlier in the book. She was better.

The interesting part of this story was that Sid stayed in this town for a week, and the surly waitress came back after a few days asking if she could try it again, This time, she did it beautifully, kindly, and without flaw. You see, when she discovered how she was, she didn't need much help. She already had an archetype of how she wanted to be. She knew what a good waitress was. She had just made the simple mistake of thinking she was one. Her defenses clouded her vision.

Change was then easy. Sid was able to come at her sideways in a startling way that let her gain new insights into her behavior by reframing the problem. Once she understood what she was doing wrong, she adjusted it. Very few people want to be bad at what they do.

# # #

Reframing works based on a set of principles in psychology that are best described by Perceptual Control Theory. For those of you who want to learn more about Perceptual Control Theory, one of the leading academic authors is man by the name of William T. Powers and his major but somewhat academic book is <u>Making Sense of Behavior.</u> A more popular presentation, more readable, is by E. Perry Good. She wrote many accessible books. A good introduction is in a volume called <u>In Pursuit of Happiness.</u>

Perceptual control theory holds that people do not like an imbalance between the picture of where they want to be and where they are presently. Earlier psychologists described a similar imbalance as 'cognitive dissonance". Some researchers have reported that many different varieties of neurosis spring from cognitive dissonance. If people see clearly where they are, and, they see clearly where they want to be, and, they wish to close the gap, they generally will move in the direction of where they want to be, or certainly, can be coached to do so.

At first glance, this seems frightfully simple. It is not.

As we discussed earlier, it is very difficult for people to assess accurately where they are presently. How many diets have failed because the morbidly obese person says him or her self, "I am not <u>that</u> fat."

How many of us have encountered the man who all evidence to the contrary says, "I am not that grumpy", or "I don't drink that much", or "I am not drowning in denial", the man said while swimming poorly in a prominent river in Egypt.

Clearly, also, some people have not defined carefully where they want to be. The old expression, 'if you're not sure where you're going, any road will get you there", holds true.

Fran counsels school principals and superintendents, professionally. In his practice, he works with people who manage multi-million dollar budgets, sometimes hundreds of millions of dollars. He cannot believe how many of them have failed to develop a personal financial plan. Many wait until they are in their late 50s before they begin to think about how much money they will need in retirement. Many over rely on credit cards, sometimes paying twice the value of what they bought, over a five-year period, when interest is considered. They pay off that item, at a great cost, that they bought, because of a wonderful sale.

They are not different from other people. Many of us repeatedly make this mistake. It is just surprising that people don't have a clear vision of where they are, and where they want to be, and a path of how they are going to get there.

Fran often makes the argument, to a disbelieving audience, that being rich is simply a decision a person has to make when they are young. Ultimately, the small decision between a tuna sandwich you bring from home and a steak you buy at a trendy restaurant contributes, over 30 years, when combined with thousands of other decisions of a similar nature, to whether you die with money in the bank, or whether you struggle through your last 10 years of life. If a person were clear where they wanted to be, financially, and understood how their decisions contribute to that outcome, they could achieve the outcome, with some discipline and dedication, regardless of what their income was.

Most people want to be rich. The problem is they also want a steak dinner. The problem is these can be competing interests.

In this country, we argue that we have a drug crisis. We have a shortage of investment capital. We have an obesity problem. We have too many alcoholics, too many unwed mothers, too much juvenile delinquency, too much drunk driving, and too much crime...In actuality, we have a single problem. We have a decision making crisis. When you don't know where you are going, any road will get you there; even, a road that we can all agree goes in the wrong direction.

People don't take the time to determine where they are. They don't take the time to develop a clear view of what they want. Without these, people can't get there.

Without a plan, based on a clear outcome, and a clear sense of our present behavior, any road will do. These social problems stem from poor decision-making based on haphazard goals or and/or faulty self pictures.

Reframing can provide rare moments of insight to people to help them to locate themselves in the change process.

To improve customer relations, we need a clearer sense of where we are going and where we are now.

# # #

A reframing moment is a moment of singular clarity. In that reframing moment, we see simultaneously where we are and where we want to be. It causes us to challenge our assumptions. It is, whether for a person, a group, or an organization, a time when we shift our method of thinking from a cyclical non-productive pattern to a new and more productive pattern. Often, the reframing moment requires a catalyst. A top-notch customer service person can reframe an issue for a customer and provide new insight. We will provide a number of reframing moments through stories so that the reader can identify a reframing event when it occurs. Lets begin:

# # #

The grandmother had called the school principal. She was unhappy because her grandchild had stated that she had had a few bad experiences with a teacher; we will call Ms. Smith. The grandmother first explained what happened in each of the incidents involving Ms. Smith.

The principal gently reminded the grandmother that sometimes the stories told by grandchildren don't line up with the facts. She indicated that she would investigate the matter and would get back to the grandmother.

The grandmother was not entirely happy. "Did the principal know," the grandmother thought silently "that this was her precious grandchild? Did she know that this teacher was mean?"

"How could she be so stupid?" The only correct response for the principal to make is that she was going to bang Ms. Smith over the head, symbolically, if not in actual practice. Grandma had to get this principal's mind right. The principal already had some learning to do, and, she would set the principal straight."

The grandmother told all four stories again. The principal thanked her and told her once again that he would speak to the teacher. The principal tried to bring the conversation to a close.

The grandmother was pretty clear that the principal did not fully understand her, if the principal did, she clearly would bang this teacher over the head. So she proceeded to explain the four stories again.

Have you ever been there, when a customer won't stop explaining the problem? You have budgeted 10 minutes for the encounter. You are a half hour into it, and there is no end in sight!

Grandma decided to launch into the problems her grandchild had with other teachers earlier and scout troop leaders and....

The principal remembered in this story something he had learned from Fran, who first learned it from Sid. The principal addressed the grandmother, "Do you mind if I get started on this right away? I've got some time available now and I would really like to jump in on this problem right away."

(What was she going to do? Could she say, "Yes, I mind. Don't get started on this right away." Of course, she wouldn't do that.)

Instead she said, "No you go right ahead. I am going to the store but I will be back by three o'clock. Give me a call. Let me know what comes of it. Thank you, Madame Principal."

Why was this a reframing event? The grandmother viewed this encounter as a time she needed to complain endlessly. She was concerned that no other behavior would get the result she wanted. Her continued complaining had worked in the past. Eventually, the people she complained to, got to it. She assumed it was the endless nature of her complaint that achieved her success. Big problems required big complaining.

Her view seemed to be that the more she complained, the more likely it was, that the principal would go along with her. She was unsympathetic to the principal's need to investigate. (She already knew the facts.) She was unconcerned with the teachers' rights. It was her grandchild's rights that were important. Grandma was waiting to hear what kind of punishment he was going to deliver to the teacher, and, Grandma probably wanted her grandchild placed in another room.

She just ground people down. She was good at it if it worked.

This caused a real intellectual/emotional knot. The principal could not punish the teacher without investigating. These situations are not always what they appear to be, the principal knew.

The encounter needed a new frame of reference. The principal provided it when she asked, "Do you mind if I get started on that right away?" Suddenly, the grandmother was reminded gently, (with a sort of twinkle in the principal's eye), that the principal needed time to resolve the problem; and, she was consuming too much of it. Grandma also knew that she was heard and the principal was going to <u>do</u> something. Grandma could relax until 3:00 PM.

As in most of these situations, other formulations of the question could also work. For example, he could have said, 'I have one hour in my schedule to work on this problem today, and perhaps even more tomorrow. How much more time should you spend helping me to better understand your perspective on the problem, because that will have to come out of the time I have to work on it." The words themselves have no magic. Many formulations could succeed.

He did not confront her directly but asked a question with such simplicity and clarity, that she gained insight that her behavior was interfering with the satisfactory resolution of the problem..... and she let him go.

# # #

When done well, reframing leads to insight, if the person, so reframed, is capable of insight. One of Sid's earlier experiments with reframing happened when he worked in a parts store. He had sold a man a shock absorber. The man went home to install it. Installing a shock absorber is dirty, time consuming work, particularly when done at home. After several hours of dirty work, the new shocks were installed. When the man lowered the car from the jack stands, one shock absorber buckled. There was obviously a defect in that shock absorber. He was angry, and disgusted with the parts store, especially, his point of contact, the now famous Sid Hurlbert, but then, simply another sales clerk.

The car was the man's only vehicle. In order to return the shock absorber, the man had to put the vehicle back up on the jack stands, crawl under the car, put the old part back in, then drive to the part store to get a replacement part. When he entered the store, he was furious. He approached Sid seething in rage. Sid grabbed the obviously defective shock absorber, spun on his heel and hollered over his shoulder "Follow me."

As Sid strode purposely forward, the man shuffled behind. Sid walked first in one direction and then in another. He led the man on a merry chase. To a casual observer, had there been one, it would have looked like a drum major swinging a broken shock instead of a baton bouncing about the store, in a very short parade, with an out of step band member who had left his instrument at home. The client exploded in outrage. "What are you trying to pull?" Sid just grinned. Then the client began to laugh, seeing the absurdity of what had just happened. Sid smiled, and the twinkle in his eye encouraged the man to know that they could have fun, even in a tense situation. Sid had taken an enormous risk. But, the gamble resulted in a window of opportunity.

Sid said, "I am so sorry. I can see why you were so mad. I would be too. This should not have happened. Let me refund your money and give you a new shock absorber. I will upgrade the quality a notch, too."

Sid had not only retained a customer in a difficult situation but he actually had gained a friend.

Both men were in a very difficult situation. Who cannot relate to the anger of the customer? Yet, how could Sid resolve the problem to the satisfaction of the customer? If the man with the broken shock were a typical do-it-yourselfer, he had probably spent four hours installing the defective shock, removing it, and reinstalling the "worn out" shock in order to drive back to the parts store. He would now require two hours to make it right again. He had lost the better part of the day, because the $40 shock absorber he had bought was no good. Yet, Sid did not manufacture the shock absorber, nor, had the store had trouble with them before. Sid wasn't knowingly selling bad merchandise. It was one of those problems that was bound to happen once in every ten thousand sales and this day it landed on Sid and this poor unsuspecting customer. Pobody is nerfect.

Would this solution always work?....Maybe not! Could it work for anybody but Sid? Maybe not!

How could we reframe it and stay within our safety zone?

Try this: "Believe me I know how you must feel. My goal is to not just solve this problem but to delight you. I know that it is hard to imagine us delighting you after what has happened but give me a chance. Here is an idea. Why don't we take you wherever you are going, we will keep your car, we will pay to have it fixed, we will refund your money, we will upgrade your shocks to a better brand and we will give you a thirty dollar credit in our store. I truly am truly sorry."

Extreme kindness in a crisis often lets people know we heard them and that we care about them and their business. That alone, can reframe a situation, often because the customer is often concerned, at that moment, that you neither hear, nor care.

Fran had such an experience at a local Lowes home improvement store. Fran had ordered three new storm doors in April to use as screen doors in the summer. First, the store lost the order. Then, the doors came in, but they were the wrong size. Then, Lowes lost the reorder. Then, the doors came in broken. Then, they forgot to reorder.

By October, Fran had lost it. He scheduled a meeting with the store manager. The manager had researched the multiple foul ups, while waiting for Fran to drive in for his appointment. When Fran got to the store, the manager had reordered the doors in a rush order, scheduled an installation, and credited Fran's account with $700.

Now, that is reframing a problem. Fran has been a regular customer at Lowes ever since.

# # #

Sid even uses reframing in his personal life. Sid loves his dad, who truly has a kindly heart. He is fundamentally a good man but he has a tongue that sometimes spirals out of control. Sometimes, his tongue can melt the skin off a turnip. He is like a lot of men, often too grumpy.

Sid's mom is sweet as honey, sensitive and long suffering. Already, you the reader can anticipate some of the usual dramas that take place in this home. Sid's dad, who genuinely loves his wife, sometimes fires from the lip, at something unimportant, which sends her into a painful panic, causing discomfort for the whole family. This is a classic pattern for the many families that have this problem. A wall will often builds up between the father and the mother, caused by the scarring due to this repeated pattern of behavior. The defenses built up to protect everyone's feelings builds a wall that is hard to penetrate.

The children will uncomfortably endure this friction, building resentment towards the father, and finally the child may explode in anger toward the father, to protect the mother. This can, with the father's tendency to "blow off steam", result in a rebutting attack on the child, curiously by the father or the mother. The problem, which was awful, probably will get worse. These kinds of dynamics often tear families apart. The problem gets worse because the child, in defending the mother, "attacked" the father's ego. The father's defenses engage, and, given his volatile nature....,what is needed is reframing.

Lest the reader think this kind of family dynamics are unusual, they probably describe the family dynamics of between 25% and 40% of families.

For two million years, natural selection favored aggressive men. Struggling in the caves of a more primitive era, families valued men who easily angered, jumped to their feet, grabbed a long spear and thrust it at invading animals or people. Aggression in men, the larger of our species, was a crucial necessary ingredient in our early family survival.

Most of us probably owe the survival of our genetic line to the existence of an aggressive male ancestor, at sometime, in the long history of our family. Fortunately, for most of us, such aggression is no longer needed, or desired, but, as we have learned, old genetic tendencies did not arrive in a single day, nor will they disappear in a single day. (None of this discussion is meant to forgive such verbal violence, not to mention any explicitly illegal acts of physical violence.)

As a species, we have more funny genetic wiring, than most of us are likely to admit. (Sid and Fran for example, have a tendency to pack on the pounds. Back when food was scarce, or even when food was available, it came intermittently. The ability to store food energy as fat was a key to their ancestor's survival. It's not working real well for either of them right now, though. There are plenty of other examples of traits that our ancestors needed to be successful, that do not work as well for us today. However, genes are genes. They don't change quickly.)

Sid knew that confronting his dad, every time that he barked at his mom, was not an effective solution to the problem. Experience had taught this. It felt good to confront his dad. Sid would be cloaked in righteousness every time he confronted his father. However, it neither improved his father's behavior, nor did it improve Sid's family dynamics.

Sid's father knew that he, the father, was a grump. He didn't understand the mechanics of his personality, that caused him to be this way; but, he knew. More than anything else in his life, he wanted to become Fred McMurray in "Father Knows Best", the kind loving dad. He couldn't admit that he was not who he wanted to be. Who wants to acknowledge, that some times they are mean to their family. This is how defenses get in the way.

Sid's dad was not happy with his impatience, and his belittling behavior. Knowing this did not help, however. When people confronted him with his behavior, he would, of course, exercise his complete set of defensive behaviors, which always were aggressive, making matters worse, and he knew this, too somewhere deep in his soul. But, he could not seem to help himself.

Sid's dad had a clear vision of where he wanted to be. He just had a hard time seeing how the present moment was related to that vision. He needed to be reminded, in a non-threatening way, that his behavior was out of bounds. The threat would bring about the exact kind of behavior he was trying to overcome.

One day, Sid's parents were taking him to the airport. They love to support Sid and his career. His mom and dad had organized quite a few happy errands around the trip to the airport. After they dropped off Sid, they were going to stop and pay some bills, pick up some things they needed, and return home full of accomplishments. There was no real time pressure, after they dropped off Sid, but true to type, Sid's dad was self-pressured to move ahead briskly. He was on the edge of impatience, as they left the driveway.

About a mile from the house, Sid's mom began to shuffle through her purse. It was the kind of purse that Kansas could have been placed in and still have had room for Rhode Island. She shuffled through the purse for probably 45 seconds with her face looking more, and more worried, each second. Finally, Sid's dad exploded. "What are you doing?" he screamed.

Timidly, she muttered, "I think I left the checkbook home."

Sid's dad's face contorted with rage, "How could you be so stupid? You would leave your head home if it were not attached. I cannot believe..."

Sid's first instinct was to say, "I think I will get out here. It is eight miles to the airport but I think I can walk that far, carrying these two heavy bags and this projector". This was a classic flight response, from the old flight or fight responses that we have "wired-in".

His next impulse was to confront his dad head-on. His dad was clearly out-of-line. This was a classic fight response. Moral indignation always feels good. Lecturing someone else about his or her bad behavior always gives us a sense of moral superiority.

However, it rarely works. It usually just raises the defensiveness of the person we have admonished. The problem becomes clearer for us when we pause for a moment to think about how we feel when someone else lectures us about our bad behavior. (And, we are not sure about the reader's behavior, but if the reader has no "bad" behavior", Sid and Fran have enough to loan the reader some of their surplus bad behavior.)

These are very difficult situations. When a pattern has repeated itself for 30 or 40 years, responding to it, as you always have, is unlikely to bring any different results from the results already obtained. Whether it is _this_ pattern of behavior; or some other patterns of behavior, we often find ourselves playing out a drama not so different from this one. Sid has a highly developed ability to reframe problems for people. This time it would be different.

"Mom," Sid admonished, "How could you do this to dad? You are always doing this kind of thing. I saw you at home, slyly pulling your checkbook from that purse and hiding it under the lamp. Why do you do these things to dad?"

"Sid," his dad hollered in reply. "Your mother would do no such thing. How could you say such a thing? She wouldn't leave the checkbook home, on purpose." Sid's father paused... looked embarrassed... and began to laugh. He had just made Sid's point. Sid's dad was caught. He realized instantly how stupid he had been for attacking his wife over this simple mental lapse. Yet, his defenses had not been raised. The older couple began to giggle like children in the front seat of the car. No further words needed to be said. The father had gained insight. He adjusted his attitude and had his temper in check, at least for this day.

Reframing can work at home as well as at work.

# # #

I hope these examples are beginning to make a pattern. Reframing brings insight, often in a potentially tense situation, by "coming up sideways" on a person, instead of hitting it "head-on". Here is another example.

Fran's mom had had rheumatic fever as a child. This resulted in a bad heart valve, which resulted in heart valve replacement surgery, which resulted in a series of strokes. Each stroke took a little bit away from his mom. The word lamb, for example, could frequently be substituted for any word, whatsoever. It was, for her the "go to" word. It could mean anything at all. "Get me the lamb" could mean get me the car keys, get me my tea, or get me the TV guide.

Her ability to sequence simple steps in a familiar process disappeared. So, she would sometimes put the tea bag in the cup, put the cup and tea bag together in the microwave for two minutes then add cold water. She lost her ability to understand time. Relative position of events lost their meaning, entirely. Her balance was compromised. Her speech was badly effected. Even some of Fran's brothers and sisters could not understand what she was saying, when she spoke.

The series of strokes presented all kinds of challenges to the entire family. Fran's dad, like Sid's, tended toward impatience. He genuinely loved his wife but was frustrated that some of the familiar patterns of their life, that he had come to depend on, were shattered by her disability. Others could no longer see Fran's mom as an intellectual equal because her ability to express herself, one of the ways we measure intelligence, had diminished, dramatically. Still others were so overcome with pity toward this wonderful woman, they could no longer treat her as a peer.

The situation needed to be reframed. The family needed a metaphor to cope with the changes in their family that her health issues had caused.

"I've got it," Fran said aloud to no one in particular, "We will begin to think of her as a dotty British eccentric. You know how in those old movies, the older British aristocrats are always doing weird things. No one resents them for it. They just act weird and then carry the title of eccentric like it is a badge of honor. You know, 'come meet my mom, she is a little weird; but, that is what is so cool about her. She is eccentric, not brain damaged."

It didn't work for everyone in the family. Fran's dad continued to be too irritable. Others in the family found it to be more or less helpful. For Fran and his wife, Lisa, it was the key to their relationship with his mom. They didn't fall into the old traps of irritability, or condescension. Her last years on earth were among the best years for Fran's relationship with his mom. Clearly, this was, purely, because the situation was reframed.

One final example:

One day when we were writing this book, it was a sunny Friday. Fran was working in the back of the house. The neighbors had hired a pretty rough crew to paint their (the neighbor's) house.

All morning the painters had played a particularly gritty kind of rock and roll music. The music just did not improve the act of writing, for Fran.

Yet, this bunch would not have responded well to "turn that damned thing down," or "change the channel". The dimensions of their defenses were unpredictable, at best. Fran was pulling out some of the last strands of hair he had left.

His wife Lisa is a natural reframer. She approached the painters, who were not nearly done with the paint job, and would clearly be working late that day.

"Thanks for providing the music this morning," she said. 'I'd like to make the selections this afternoon. If you would turn your boom box down, I'll crank mine up. You can try my tunes this afternoon. At the end of the day, let's compare notes."

They turned theirs down. Ella Fitzgerald came up. The music for the rest of the day helped the writing. Her approach was for more effective than an approach that attacked their rock and roll.

Reframing sometimes is the only way to effectively resolve a problem, and, as you will soon see, it can be the key to improving customer service.

# # #

Some who read this book already have a gift in helping others to reframe difficult situations. Most of us could stand to improve our skills in this area. The problem is that these are not skills, like long division, that can be easily taught in isolation, and then combine to make the student competent. We will, however, do our best to break the steps down to make success at reframing more probable. The remainder of this book will attempt to analyze and teach the components of reframing. AND how to apply them.

#

In breaking down the components of the reframing process, we have developed an acronym, CUSTOMER. The components of reframing are:

- **C**aution signals alert us, indicating that this is a problem that calls out for reframing.

- **U**nderstand, at a profound level, the true dynamics of the situation.

- **S**tartle yourself, and others, with a fresh approach.

- **T**est your ideas against the facts.

- **O**riginality and humor help here.

- **M**ake it non-confrontational.

- **E**xercise your risk-taking.

- **R**oll It Out

We will take you through these steps. Perhaps the acronym will help you to remember them, when you are in a situation that requires reframing.   It is a lot to remember but, what Sid and Fran have learned, is that once you have tried reframing a few times successfully it can become a tool that you can count on.

C — CAUTION SIGNALS ALERTS US, INDICATING THAT THIS IS A PROBLEM THAT CALLS OUT FOR REFRAMING.

People don't need to reframe every decision that they face. Most of what we do in life is automatic, or nearly automatic, and this is helpful.   Deciding whether to use a fork or spoon to eat a cream soup should probably not require a tremendous amount of mental energy.

Maybe, if we were in the food business, that question could trigger a creative and perhaps profitable new insight, but as a guest at Sid's house on Tuesday, it would be a diversion that could consume precious time, and move us nowhere.

There are, however, situations that call out for reframing. Knowing when to use this tool is the first step. We need to learn to recognize them. There are always knots. These are complex problems, difficult to untie.

In our lives, there are many times that our logic becomes circular and we get a bad result. An example taken from the parenting of teens might be helpful here.

Teenagers often get in a cycle of bad behavior. This usually starts when a teenager has a mild bump, like getting a bad grade on a report card. As loving parents, we might, in an effort to set limits for our child, tell a teenager in such a bind that they are grounded for a month. The teenager, feeling badly about the report card, and that they had disappointed mom and dad, might also be angry because they can't, now, see their boyfriend/girlfriend. A fight response might kick in from our old fight or flight tapes. In an effort to strike back, the teen might not come home from school one day, go to a friend's house, and return home only to face a new punishment which might them to be grounded for another month.

Their frustration and anger might cause them to swear at their parent, which would cause them to be grounded for another month. (Fight or flight) The frustration and anger from the incidents above might cause them to smuggle alcohol in the house, and....

No parental response in the above example was absolutely wrong by itself. Kids need limits. For most of us, behaviors should lead to consequences, positive and negative. Consistency is important.

But, oops! Something went wrong here. However logical, kind, and thoughtful, the parent in this story may have thought himself or herself to be, this situation is going nowhere. This is a classic knot. The patterns that we use to solve problems are not working and going nowhere.

The situation calls out for reframing. This is not a book on parenting. This section is to help you how to identify when reframing is needed. Here, there is a solution that has been tried, and tried again. It simply has not worked. Soon the rebellion, at hand, is going to boil over. Some parents would just continue to punish into compliance. Could it work? It is a test of wills. We see a pattern. Certainly there is a risk in simply applying the same solution, which has not gotten results, over and over. .

Fran raised a lot of children, not all of whom were his own. As a school superintendent, he was often in a position to catch kids, who were in a free fall. He used to buy Monopoly games at garage sales just to take the "get out of jail free" cards for these occasions. When repeated punishments failed and kids were locked in a downward spiral he would take out his wallet, and with a great florish, issue the "get out of jail free card to the student, explains he was free to go and recalibrate the relationship."

When you are doing some things repeatedly that just do not work; do something else.

These knots or puzzles happen more frequently than you might imagine. Sometimes they represent lifelong patterns of behavior. When someone is trapped in one of these knots, their ability to choose an effective new behavior from a wide repertoire of behaviors, diminishes. When watching one of these situations, one gets the sense that they are watching a drama play out that is almost written by someone else. Like, in a good knot, there seems to be no place to reach in and pull the strands apart.

What does this have to do with customer service?

We have used several examples in the last few pages that are readily identifiable, that are knots or puzzles. Do you remember the case of the grumpy waitress? Sid went into a restaurant for breakfast. The waitress came over and snarled "What do you want?" her mannerisms were hostile. The experience was unpleasant. Her behavior made prefect sense to her. She never challenged her own thinking. There was an internal logic, "I may have to wait on these people but I don't have to like it."

The internal logic propelled the behavior. It was like a drama written by someone else. The actual logic of her behavior was counter productive. The underlying true logic ought to have been, "I work for tips; I ought to 'suck up' to these people." Or, "it is a privilege to serve people." Or, "I can make their day." Or, "Through my outstanding service, I can make this company thrive." Or, if I am kind and helpful, people will love me and I will be happier. These were clearly not what was on her mind.

From the outside, we can all see that the logic of these later pieces of "self-talk" would simply work better for the waitress. If she could learn to value customer service and permit that value to change her behavior, her job would be more secure. Her boss would be happier. She would get more tips. Her day would fly by. Her work would feel lighter. <u>And</u>, she would be happier. Not only, would this commitment to personal service, bring all customers would provide her constant "strokes". She would get great feedback. As Sid has said earlier in the book, "The most important reason to give great customer service is that it feels good."

This woman has her logic clearly in a knot. Her attitude has imprisoned her from seeing reality clearly. Sid's reframing remark, "I'll have another waitress" came up along her sideways. It alerted her to the problem without raising her defenses.

The guy with the shock absorber was also about to enter a huge knot. Remember him, from earlier in the book? He was a do it yourself mechanic who bought a shock absorber from Sid. When he installed it, it buckled. He had to put the old on in to get back to the store to complain. This doubled the time he had in the project. And, still he had a broken shock. He didn't know how Sid would handle it. Faced with overwhelming disappointment and unhappiness, old tapes from infancy began to take over his behavior.

When an infant is tired, hungry, sick, cold, hot, sore, wet or lying in fecal material, the infant responds with a generalized body spasm. It is often involuntary. He or she becomes wracked with tears.

Over time, children learn that this generalized response also brings a generalized and not specific response from the adult. Tears over a safety pin stuck in the infant's side can bring warm bottle of milk instead of the relief the infant seeks. So, children learn, over time, to be more specific about what concerns them; and to approach the adults in their environment using methods that bring them the results they want ever more effectively.

However, when faced with profound disappointment the old tapes often play in our heads, and we respond like an infant, merely expressing our pain with a generalized full body response.

The customer could have been more effective by raising his concerns differently. "Sid, I have just had an experience that is so painful to me, that I am likely to behave rather badly. Sid, think of yourself as a contestant in the national customer service quiz show. You need an A+ response on this customer service challenge in order to move into the million dollar round...Are you ready Sid? I've got one heck of a story for you."

He did not. He just went crazy.

This would have been an example of the customer reframing the situation for the customer service representative if he had. And, it would have worked.

The point is that the old tape, the infancy whine, is not a particularly productive tape. It often creates an example of a knot or puzzle that calls out for reframing.

So, the first step in using reframing effectively is to understand when to use it. We don't use it to handle everyday routine problems. Life should not demand that kind of creativity and mental energy every minute of every day. Reframing provides people with an opportunity to see a complex problem in a fresh perspective. When a person, group, or organization is "stuck" in a non-productive bit of circular reasoning, or when they exhibit behaviors that make sense to them but don't make sense, in the absolute, they may be in a knot or puzzle.

When people are locked in a non-productive self-reinforcing set of behavior that simply don't work, reframing may be helpful. That is why we say, "Caution signals alerts us, indicating that this is a problem that calls out for reframing." Knowing when to use reframing is the first step to using it effectively.

U — Understand, at a profound level, the true dynamics of the situation.

Through reframing, people gain insights into their present behavior, or gain insights of what they want to achieve.

Once they understand what they want to achieve, and understand where they are now, they can move to close the gap. In order to assist them in gaining this insight, it is helpful, if the person reframing has a deeper insight into the underlying dynamics of what is going on. Situations are not always as they present themselves. There are often underlying issues that are different from the presenting situation.

The diabetic came into a particular discount department store late in the evening. She had asked to return her glucometer. (The glucometer is a portable electronic device that measures sugar in the blood.) The clerk went to his keyboard to enter the return. A note came up on his computer screen indicating that because this product used needles to get blood samples, it could not be returned. He informed her that she could not get a replacement, and that he could not repair or receive this device that night.

Behind the clerk, above the desk, was a blue sign that stated all products sold at this particular store, which were defective, would be replaced or repaired by the company.

The conversation that followed was ugly. The diabetic kept pointing to the sign. The clerk kept saying that he was not permitted to return this product without an approval from the computer. She began to rant and rave about a store run by a computer. Customers were beginning to gather in a semi-circle, partly for the entertainment value, and partly out of shock and horror, for what had become a truly ugly scene. The manager of the store was drawn by the commotion near the return desk.

He approached the scene confidently, extended his hand to the customer and said, "I am Neil Rochelle. I am the manager of the store. May I help you?"

"I hope so," she fired back. "This sorry ass shit for brains clerk can't read his own sign. It says we will fix or replace any broken stuff. I bought this glucometer today when my old one wore out. I have the receipt. It never worked once. I need a new one, now."

This was a critical moment. Neil knew that. The crowd had gathered, the employee wanted to be supported, the women was in crisis. Neil's first instinct was to give this woman a lesson about her foul mouth. His blood pressure had immediately gone up, because of her assault on his employee. The clerk was not a brain surgeon, but he was a nice enough kid. Everywhere there is an "us" and "them" mentality. In this case, the "us" was the store employees and "them" was the customers. Neil could clearly see already that this approach was going to go nowhere. He knew that a instinctive response here was only going to escalate the crisis and cause further problems. He had mastered the C of our acronym *CUSTOMER*. Caution signals had gone up. He was now seeking to Understand, our U in *CUSTOMER*.

"What is a glucometer?" he asked innocently.

"It is a 'thing-a-bob' I use to measure my blood sugar," she replied.

"Are you a diabetic?" Neil asked.

"Yes, damn it," she spurted.

"That must be difficult," Neil sympathized.

"You have no idea," she said. She breathed a little easier. At last, someone was listening.

"So help me to understand what is going on?" he asked in a concerned voice.

"My sugar levels have been bouncing all over the place. I thought it was me, but when my old glucometer finally wore out, I began to wonder if the glucometer was the problem. I bought this new one today; and, before I even got one reading, it turned up busted, and this jerk told me I can't return it. I spent my last dollar on it. I'm stuck, and I am worried about my blood sugar. I have not had a good reading in weeks. I could be in a real health crisis."

The required level of understanding had now been achieved. Neil had dug a little deeper than the clerk had. He knew now, what the underlying dynamic was. The people, who had gathered simply to watch the show, were drifting away. Two people were now talking, not two adversaries. Neil had connected with the customer. Neil now had the opportunity to solve the problem.

"What is your name?" Neil asked. He was moving away from an adversary relationship further and toward a more personal one.

"Ruth", she said.

"Ruth, he addressed her, "Peter here is not a bad kid. He is certainly not a jerk. We don't get problems like this very often, and frankly, we are going to learn from this and change our policy. I am concerned about your health. You need to get an accurate reading tonight. Don't you?"

"Yes", she said with a sense of relief. She had finally been heard.

"Peter, you go get Ruth a new one of these off the shelf, unless you would rather have a different brand, Ruth", Neil asked.

"No", Ruth said thoughtfully. "I have been reading about these, I think I just got a bad one."

"Peter, go and get that. We will give it to Ruth. Ruth, I don't know how we will sort this out tomorrow, but I want you to keep the bad one, too. Bring the bad one back tomorrow, and we will figure out what to do with it. I will be in at noon and I will call headquarters to sort out what we will do. They are not open tonight. I will work until closing tomorrow night. You can come in anytime after about 1:00 PM. We may end up sending it back to the company, but I will know that tomorrow before you get here. These things are so reliable that we have never had this come up before. I am sure Peter agrees with me, the most important thing we can do tonight is to make sure you get the information you need to manage your diabetes, right, Peter?"

"Absolutely," Peter responded.

By now, the last of the assembled crowd was drifting away. If anything, Ruth had become a more committed customer. Peter felt supported, and Neil was able to go home feeling good about himself, his company, and the level of service he had provided. He had a story to tell his wife and his children. The reason for all of this good feeling came from his ability to understand the underlying dynamic, not merely the presenting dynamic.

> It was presented as an "us" vs. "them" power struggle about company regulations and policies, but, it was a health crisis, assisted by an empowered and understanding employee.

> "Seek first to understand, then to be understood", the St. Francis Prayer teaches us.

This story is beautiful; however, it is not true. In the true story, Fran, our author, was Ruth. No manager appeared. The computer was in charge, and with his blood sugar screaming out of control at 9:55 PM with no other possibility to buy a glucometer; he left the store with no resolution to his health problem, short of going to the emergency room of the local hospital. Fran did not shop again in this store for many years.

The crowd that gathered around the explosive vignette probably contained a few people, who, horrified at the insensitivity of Peter, and thereby the store, probably also stopped shopping there.

Like most wronged customers, Fran proceeded to tell the story to his friends and relatives with increasing emotion; and, they too, probably reduced their frequency of shopping at the store. The reason for the store's policy probably makes sense. Who wants to accept return products with the potential for dirty needles?

Even Fran would argue that handling dirty needles is a bad idea; and that generally, glucometers are very reliable. This problem is quite rare, and I am sure the store sees the problem very infrequently and almost never at closing time. Perhaps, it is the only time it has ever happened.

In the true story, all parties lost. No one reframed the issue. No one attempted to Understand.

The next day, Fran called the manufacture of the glucometer. He mailed it back to them, and they sent him a new one. He bought a second one from a local drug store to fill the gap. He happily paid more than the discount department store price, rather than returning to that store to buy a second one. He now has a spare.

The store lost probably $2000 in gross sales each year from Fran, alone, without the damage that he spread, by telling this story to others. Wouldn't it be nice if Neil actually existed and truly understood?

# # #

Even Neil Rochelle cannot resolve every situation. Sometimes customers are just plain crazy. (Lets hope Fran is not.) Sometimes there is no solution.

Here is a problem with a happy ending. When Fran taught at a college. He is now a Dean. A foreign gentleman was pacing back and forth outside his open door loudly huffing and puffing as Fran was trying to teach one day during the summer session in May. Fran started the students on a case study; left the classroom, gently closed the door, and asked the man if he could help him. The man exploded in rage. "Where is the graduation?" the man asked in a heavily accented voice. "This is Saturday, today is graduation. Where is it?"

"What graduation?" Fran asked gently.

"This is St. John Fisher College?" the man asked....

"Yesssss.....?" Fran said cautiously.

"My son said graduation was today," the man asserted.

Graduation had been the previous weekend. It had been a glorious affair. St. John Fisher College does graduations well. There were balloons, and speeches, and food in abundance. There was a sea of happy faces.

Fran wondered, could this poor guy have gotten his dates wrong. Did he come from out-of-town to attend a graduation on a wrong weekend? Fran thought to himself, "Poor son-of gun. He missed a good one."

"No sir, graduation was last week."

"How could that be?", he asked. "My son told me it was today. "

"I am very sorry you missed it. It was a great occasion. Did your son graduate?" asked Fran seeking to understand. The caution warning had already gone off.

"No, and that is the problem. He was supposed to graduate. He has been coming to this college for four years, and he was supposed to graduate. This place always gives me the run around. I have come here to finally track down somebody who can tell me why he is not graduating. He says it is because he got a C minus on one course and the College is making him come back for one whole year. This College is so stupid. How could they do that to my boy?" he hollered shaking with rage.

The students in Fran's class would soon be finished with their review of the case study.

This was an enormous problem that no doubt would require hours of resolution. It was unraveling unpleasantly in the hallway outside Fran's room. This encounter took place at about 11:00 AM. The class that day would last until at least 3:OO PM. It would do no good to explain to this gentleman that the college was a good place, that the college took good care of its students, and that the problem was probably more complex than he was led to believe.

Instead, Fran reached into his wallet, took out a business card, and said to the man, "My name is Dr. Murphy, I teach here. You have come to the right place. Let's work on this together. Let's try to find out what went wrong. We will need access to your son's records and he will have to provide us that access. Come to my office. We will write a release that will give permission for you and I to review his records.

"Bring your son on Monday with the release at 11:00 to this office and we will go together to the registrar's office to find out what happened. If something outrageous has happened to your son, I will go with you to the proper College official's office and we will straighten it out. I will set up an appointment at the President's Office, in case we need it," Fran concluded.

A lot more needed to be done to fully understand the problem. But the problem, as presented, "Where's the graduation ceremony?" was not the problem. The problem was that this man felt the College had unfairly denied his son his diploma.

Fran did not respond to the problem presented. He responded to the underlying problem. Fran knew that there was more to the problem than the Dad understood. Fran suspected that the man's son had been misleading him. He could not untangle that situation this day. But, he could show the father that the College was not insensitive and that he, the father, was not without resources, or support from the College. The father left, confident that the situation would be resolved, with a plan of action. At last, he had been heard.

Of course, later the father would learn in the Registrar's Office that the student had failed numerous courses and also failed to tell his father the truth. The subsequent meetings were fascinating. The father's respect for the College was restored. The boy had a lot of explaining to do.

The problem presented, is often not the problem. The first step in this process, was

"Caution signals alert us indicating that this is a problem that calls out for reframing." We will hence forth abbreviate this step to the single word, "Caution".

The two presenting situations in this section (the diabetic, in the first incidence; and, the angry father in the second) clearly called out for a different response than an ordinary one. A bell should have gone off in the head of the person with the customer service opportunity, to reframe this problem.

Without this new level "Understanding" progress cannot be made. It is a critical step in the reframing process.

It shouldn't take a crisis for a company to push the "U" button. There are more systemic reasons for companies to use their instinct to understand the dynamics of the customer at a profound level.

Jack Helfrich was Superintendent of Schools in the Kenmore-Tonawanda School District in suburban Buffalo, New York. He was celebrated for the high level of achievements of his school district. He was selected New York State Superintendent of the Year and won New York Stare Excelsior Award for product quality competing against New York's many quality industries.

Jack had a lot of "secrets" to his success. One was very simple and very effective. Each of his managers (principals, assistant principals, assistant superintendents, and the superintendent himself) were tasked with the responsibility to call five "customers" every week, selected at random from the list of parents in the school system. They asked the same two questions every week. The conversation went as follows:

"Good morning, Mrs. Smith. This is Jack Helfrich. I am the Superintendent here in Kenmore-Tonawanda, and, there is nothing wrong with Tommy. I try to call five parents a week to get parents' ideas of what we are doing right and how we could improve. Do you have a few minutes to talk to me today?"

(First of all, how is Jack doing? Has he impressed Mrs. Smith already? Has your child's superintendent called you this week to seek your feedback and input to improve the school system? Has his approach already startled Mrs. Smith with his commitment to customer service?)

"I have a few minutes," Mrs. Smith said tentatively.

"How are we doing for Tommy?" Jack would ask. After her reply, Jack would follow up, "Are there ways that we could serve you or Tommy better? Do you have any suggestions for ways we could improve? Are there things we are doing well that we ought to continue to do? Is there something we are doing now that we could do more of? Do you have any other thoughts for us?"

After completing the conversation and taking notes throughout, Jack would thank Mrs. Smith for sharing her ideas and providing ways that the school system could improve. The notes from all the administrators would be submitted in rough form every week to Jack's secretary where they would all be typed, distributed to the administrative team, and would become the first item of business on the monthly administrative team meetings.

The time commitment on this task was minimal. Each administrator had to make one call a day. Jack's secretary had about two hours each week to collect and type the notes. Each month about one half hour to forty-five minutes was devoted to understanding "the welcome voice of the customer." The benefits were enormous.

# # #

S — Startle yourself with a fresh approach.

The two reasons for reframing are that you "come up along side" someone instead of hitting him or her head on; and, "to think outside the box"

There is a discipline to creativity. Here is an example:

> Fran used to enter the National Pun Contest every year. In order to do that you had to be able to write an extended pun. At first this seems a daunting challenge. Actually, writing a pun is pretty easy once you know the system.

Most puns end after a long story with a slightly mangled popular expression. So Fran always began with a popular expression. Here is one of his best or worst puns, depending on your point of view:

> *Edgar Allen Poe was a great writer. He also used a lot of drugs. During his time, "laughing gas" was invented. Poe was dying to try it. So he made an arrangement to buy a balloon full of laughing gas for two hundred dollars. The night for the delivery came. The seller of laughing gas came to the house with a tuba case. Inside the tuba case was to be a balloon full of laughing gas. Poe was to have the laughing gas inhaled from the balloon. Poe paid the man two hundred dollars. The man opened the tuba case but the balloon had burst. The gas had escaped.*
>
> *Poe snatched back his money and said, "Do not gas Poe. Do not collect two hundred dollars."*

Isn't it amazing that Fran did not get even an honorable mention for that groaner.

How did he write it? He began with the monopoly expression "Do not pass go. Do not collect two hundred dollars." He was prepared to trade some letters around and wanted a story that would get him there. That is how you write a pun

Given a half a bottle of bourbon and three idle hours, almost anyone can do it. Creativity often seems like a mundane act. It is not. A careful reading of this section will help you be more systematic about your creativity.

How does one startle oneself with a fresh approach to a seemingly intractable problem?

Of course, you begin by identifying the problem (caution), and then you seek to understand the true dynamics underlying the problem (understand). Now the creative work begins. Creativity is merely the combination of two things that are not ordinarily combined. Let's review some of the examples we have already used. When the waitress approached Sid, to ask rudely, "What do you want?" Sid's "caution" signal already went off. He knew that this woman was locked in a frequently repeated pattern. He also knew he did not want to continue to support it. His "understanding" was immediate. This is a grumpy lady who really doesn't want to help me. His "startle" response was really quite simple. He took her question literally. "What do you want?"

"I want a new waitress."

There are many times that this approach works very easily. Fran often says, much to his own amusement, but not necessarily his wife's, to a waitress who asks, after delivering the meal, "Can I get you anything else?"

"Just your support and friendship."

When people respond to the literal question, they often startle people. We have such automatic responses to certain questions that any alternative reply brings freshness to the situation.

"How are you today?" someone asked Sid.

"Better than I deserve to be", Sid replies frequently.

"How are you today?" someone asks Fran.

"I am having more fun than I have pockets to put it in", Fran replies.

Sometimes, just taking a fresh approach to the ordinary routines of life will startle people into a new perspective. Sometimes in response to the same question as "So how are you?" Fran replies, in the right country setting, among only men "Slicker than snot on a porcelain door knob, thank you."

How do these help people reframe? As a society, we are awash in pessimism.

Taking the mind out of park, and putting it into drive is often enough to cause everyone in the neighborhood to look freshly at the things that are going on in their lives. Fun is infectious. People catch it from each other, and pass it around. One person can make a difference simply by startling people with replies to common routines.

#

Fresh replies to commonplace inquiries are not the <u>only</u> way to startle. Here is a second approach that like the earlier system for writing puns can be made to be a systematic approach to startling others. Analogies and metaphors are useful to find a fresh approach. Here is a customer service example:

> The dapper gentlemen entered the downtown shoe store. He was wearing a brown suit and white and brown wing tipped shoes. His selection of tie and shirt were stunning. He was carrying a plastic bag with the name of the store on it. In the bag, was a shoe box. He walked briskly to the counter. Moments later, a clerk moved behind the counter and said, "May I help you."

> "Yes", the dapper gentlemen replied. "I bought these here. They don't fit. I would like to return them."

> The clerk opened the box, pulled the shoes out, and coolly examined them. They were quite used. The heels were worn down enough so that a careful person would have had them re-heeled. The soles were badly scuffed and worn. There were creases behind the toe cap that clearly showed a high level of use.

> _Caution_ went off in the sales clerk mind that we were about to hit a place where an old tape would replay. The clerk had been through this many times. He knew that the store owner would not accept a well worn pair of shoes back into stock. The owner could not sell a pair of worn shoes and therefore, could not take them back. The clerk knew that the scene was about to be ugly. "These shoes were worn," he would say.

> "No, they are not," would come the reply. Clearly, the clerk had an _understanding_ of the underlying dynamics.

> "Yes, they are", the clerks would reply.

"I am insulted", the man would say.

What was needed now was a way to take a fresh approach, to *startle*.

"No wonder you stay in such great shape," the clerk noted. "Those clothes hang off of you beautifully. I saw when you walked in, you really looked good. Your tailor must smile when he sells you a suit."

"Why, thank you," the gentlemen replied.

"You must really be a walker. Is that how you stay in shape?"

"Well, yes, that, and I go to the gym."

"Even though these shoes are almost new, I can't take them as a return because you are such an athletic gentleman. Your very personality wears down shoes faster than most men. I could offer you a discount on your next pair of shoes, though to compensate you for the inconvenience of these not fitting as well as they should."

"Well, thank you young man. That would be very nice," the gentleman said.

A head to head confrontation clearly does not often work. Defenses get into the way. Which of us, when we are customers, wants to be told we are lying (even when we are)? Clearly, the man had worn the shoes too much to return them. The owner would not accept used shoes back. By distracting the customer with some flattery, the clerk was able to "come up side ways" on this man instead of head-on. What could have been an ugly confrontation became a pleasant conversation. Distracting the customer by startling him or her is a good way to take the ego out of potentially ugly situations and *startle* the customer.

Startling the customer is not just a way to reframe a customer complaint, but ought to be how we do business. As was pointed out earlier in the book, customer service is not merely reactive response to customer unhappiness but ought to be a proactive ongoing, method of engaging the customer.

There has been a lot of talk in the management literature over the past two decades about exceeding customer expectations. The

Chrysler mini van must have more cup holders per square inch than any car that we have ever seen. In Fran's family, there is a mini van and a Volvo. Fran is addicted to coffee. So is his wife Lisa. They love the cup holders in their mini van.

When it came time to replace the Volvo, there was a spirited debate around the kitchen table. The arguments on the Volvo side were safety and Volvo's legendary durability. The advocate at that table for another kind of car pushed the cup holders. (Fortunately, the Volvo S80 had done a better job with cup holders than the older Volvo models.) They ended up with a Volvo, much to Fran's delight.

Isn't it interesting how a feature that "delighted" the customer like cup holders, that was invented out of whole cloth, became a new essential ingredient? In 1980, none of us knew what a cup holder was. By 2003, cup holders had become a criterion by which we select cars, a new minimum expectation.

Delighting the customer and exceeding expectations is how an organization brings the "startle" aspect of customer service into its repertoire. But, exceeding expectations is a never ending challenge because customer expectations, as we saw in the Volvo example, raise with the improvement in customer service.

In 1952, none of us "needed" air conditioning in a car. Air conditioning for most people was rolling down the windows or lowering the convertible top. Radios, in 1952 were something we had at home, predominantly; now, most of us a "need" premium audio system in a car. Most males as customers, in their twenties, seem to require a subwoofer that vibrates the chest cavity of everyone standing one block away.

Startling the customer with our customer service takes work, originality, and focus. Fran always pays too much for his groceries. As in many major markets, there are many places to buy groceries in Rochester, New York. The chain that has the best lighting, best displays, and best trained employees probably charges ten cents more per pound for everything it sells. He won't shop anywhere else. He drives right by a store from a competing chain, which, arguably, is cheaper, in order to get to "his" store. The chain he favors actually has people to help load the groceries into the car. Fran has never used their help, but, he thinks its "cool" that, if ever he needed them, they would be there. (Cher visited Rochester and approached the manager of one of these markets to ask that they open a store in her area.)

Wegmans, a Rochester favorite grocery chain, is addicting. A company that "leads" with its customer service can be outrageous. At a recent stay at a hotel, the Madison Renaissance, in Seattle, Fran called down to ask for a wake up call. The telephone operator asked, "And, how would you like your coffee, Dr Murphy?"

First, it was startling that she replied with <u>Dr</u>. Murphy. Fran does not wear his PhD like armor. He had not registered as Dr. Murphy. The desk clerk must have picked it up from the credit card used, and moved it to the telephone operator. Fran replied, "That is a little personal, isn't it? Why do you care how I take my coffee?"

"We need to know how you like your coffee so that 15 minutes before you receive your wake up call we can deliver a pot of steaming coffee outside your door, so that you can wake up to coffee and the newspaper...or would you prefer tea?"

Fran made it complicated. "I will have regular and my wife will have decaf and cream, please."

The next morning the Murphy's awoke and there was a small tray containing two full pots of coffee, regular and decaf outside their door. Fran will not stay at another hotel in Seattle. This startling free service has become a new minimum expectation, at least, while staying in Seattle.

And, what did this uncommon service cost the hotel? What percentage of the $150 per night was this startling service? Why wouldn't every hotel do this? What would it do for the mood of their customers, the morale of their staff, and the percentage of repeat business? How complicated is this?

Staff providing extraordinary service love the response they get from customers. It propels further acts of world class service. The Madison Renaissance is a place where outrageous acts of service are the norm for employees.

#

Camp Good Days and Special Times is a wonderful Rochester area camp for children and families with cancer. (It also serves families affected by Aids, violence, the death of a parent, burn victims, and ...) Fran has been a long time volunteer and a member of the board. Clearly, if any organization was to be committed to customer service, this organization should be.

Gary Mervis, the founder of the camp, clearly understood this. He ensured that the largely volunteer staff was selected and programs were designed to pack a "lifetime of fun in a single week". What does this level of customer service look like?

The commitment to children served by the camp (which is largely staffed by volunteers) results in a culture that has many startling features. Here are a few:

- Every morning a few dedicated staff members rise before every one else, to make coffee. Each cabin is awakened by a song sung by the coffee deliverers. There is a morning joke and fresh coffee for staff, and older campers.

- Among the staff, the greatest honor is to be the last served on the food line. Some staff have to eat with children, who need their company, and their assistance. But, at Camp Good Days, if you are the last to eat, it means you have given every one else what they need first. That is a good thing. It is valued in that culture. How different is this from schools, whose teachers routinely cut in line?

- When waiting in line for dinner, lunch or breakfast, strange things break out, like the back scratching activity where each person, in line, scratches the back of the person in front of them.

- Our program offerings are infinite in their variety. We don't have a bowling alley and we don't offer a program in bowling. But, if any child mentions that they would like to go bowling, we arrange it, immediately. So it is with airplane rides, hot air balloons, skin diving....

Top quality customer service is, by definition, not usual and customary. It, in fact, does delight the customer. It catches the customer by surprise. It does startle.

How does a company or an organization move into this brave new world?

Let's go to the system we already begun to develop. The first step in our acronym "CUSTOMER" was caution. The caution, here, in developing a systematic startling, high level of customer service is the caution of knowing that if you don't exceed your customer's service expectations, you will be out of business. The second step was to "understand". Understanding here means to understand customer's expectations, wants, desires, and needs. Corporation and organizations that do this well are constantly systematically engaged with their customers.

We may have it wrong, but we believe that Chrysler invented the cup holder. If so, they did not do that in isolation. They met with customers asking the customers to think "out of the box". "What bugs you as you drive to work in the morning?" "What would a car do that would delight you?" If a car could read your mind, "What would be different about it?" "Would you mind if I ride with you everywhere you go, for a few days, to watch how you use our product?" Any time you have a minor annoyance anywhere you go today, just tell me. We are trying to recreate the whole concept of "car". Engineers would ask customers these kinds of questions.

How sophisticated does this research have to be. How many customers do you have to ask? Do you have to hire someone to do this research?

Some data is better than none. That's the bottom line. If you don't ask, you won't know.

Huge national advertising campaigns are tested on focus groups of no more than 10 or 20 people. People's views, although they vary, are more alike than they are dissimilar. A small group of customers can help companies gain new insights.

I was not an insider with Chrysler on the invention of the cup holder. My fantasy is that some engineer was talking to a customer or riding with a customer in their car when the coffee spilled and the customer said ,"Damn, I hate it when my coffee mug spills when I turn suddenly." If someone had asked my father in 1952 about how he used his car and what his problems were and what annoyed him when he drove, a cup holder would have been in the 1953 Ford Fairlane.

If an organization wants to startle their customers in a systematic way, proactively, they will understand the customer's expectations, needs, wants, and the customer's minor annoyance with their products or services.

Great customer service does not just happen, nor do exhortations to improve customer relations do it alone. A company that exceeds the expectations of their customers has to want to exceed those expectations. They have to hire people who want to do it. They have to provide customers with a special experience, train their staff, and then plan specifically how exceeding customer expectations will happen. _Startling_ your customer in a world class fashion requires a world class organization, focused on the customer.

Mike Cobb at Great Peak Ski Area understood this. He knew from talking to customers that waiting in line for the lift was one of the most annoying aspects of skiing. He also knew by observing that the lines were worst from about ten o'clock in the morning until eleven thirty and then from one o'clock until about two thirty. (The problem only existed on the weekends and holidays.) He knew that at his ski area the real problem was at the main lift from his base lodge to the top of the main hill. (These observations were the most important part of finding the solution.) If waiting in lines on all lifts, at all times, were the problem, there probably were no solutions short of reducing the number of customers. . But by defining the problem in this way, the problem was bite sized.

If Mike could find a way to reduce the problem for six hours a week between December 25th and March 1st, at one ski lift, he would probably improve the customer satisfaction at his ski area by 50 percent.

Mike brought a team together to address this problem. Fran was a part of that team. The team suggested entertainment at the offending lift line during those hours…clowns, jugglers, comedians, fiddle players, and more.   The ski area did not have the margin of profitability to pay union scale for professional acts. But it did have a resource of amazing power. It had the power to give the entertainers free skiing in return for a few hours of entertaining at the lift lines.

This insight changed the quality of the experience to those of us who skied at Great Peak during those years. Were the customers startled? You bet!

Clowns, jugglers and musicians gladly traded two hours of entertaining the crowds at the lift line for a day's pass on the mountain for their family. The line got no shorter, but it felt shorter and bad performers were as good as good ones. They made it a kind of a gong show.

# # #

Oh that's all right for a ski area, but, it couldn't happen here.

Don't try to tell that to Fran Murphy. As a school superintendent, he was committed to delighting the customer. Owego, New York, at the time he became Superintendent there, was a sleepy suburb of Binghamton, New York, itself a small city. The community was divided between highly skilled, largely white-collar IBM employees, and a much more diverse, largely blue-collar and agrarian local population. The children of the IBM parents took high level courses in the high school, went to college, and did pretty well. The children of the rest of the population were too often less successful. Instructionally, the problem was to raise the expectations, and the vision of this second population, and to have everyone have fun doing it. This was accomplished in a lot of ways. We will highlight here, one of those solutions. As you read this, put it up against your experience of going to school.

The local IBM plant wanted to help advance the cause of education and had been very helpful to the school district in its efforts to move forward. The vice-president of the local plant was a very bright and capable man by the name of John Sponyoye. Fran had met with John numerous times. They had established a friendship. They had tried some projects. The projects had worked pretty well and they were now at a point to take some risks. Fran put together a team to focus on "raising the bar" and delighting the customer. The focus was math and science. That was at the insistence of IBM. This project would take place, not just in the Owego School District, but in all of the Tioga County schools.

In the elementary schools, each teacher from grades three through six was brought to an in-service training program. Each teacher was given an ESTES EGGSPRESS Rocket. These rockets were designed to take an egg off a launch pad into the sky, where a parachute would open and the egg would be brought gently back to earth. The rockets were about two feet tall. The teachers were shown how to assemble the rockets. (This is rocket science.) and they were let in on the plan, and trained how to implement it.

Each class, grade three through six would build a rocket. The custodians in each building would be trained how to launch them. The kindergarten, first and second graders would paint the rockets before the rocket engines were installed. Each school would be given a device, which used a sighting protractor, and simple trigomononetric principals, to measure of the height of the rocket path. The principal would be trained to work with sixth graders to gather this data. Half of the rockets in each school would be loaded with an egg. Half would be sent off "empty". Every classroom would be tasked with the responsibility of generating a hypothesis for which would go higher. ....the one with the egg or the one without the egg. Each teacher would bring their data from their class to a county-wide conference on science and math teaching, where the data would be entered into a computer program and a science experiment report, which included the following sections, would be printed and a copy returned to each child. The sections of the report were:

- Statement of the problem.

- Hypothesis.

- Method.

- Materials.

- Data.

- Conclusions.

For the remainder of the year, teachers would use this report format to work with the students on other scientific experiments, supplied by the consortium in little self-contained Tupperware tubs. Each summer the consortium would reload the tubs.

At the follow-up conference, which was held for all teachers in the county, for all grade levels, Jim Lovell, Commander of Apollo 13 held all the teachers spellbound as he first described the terrifying story of Apollo 13 flight and then discussed how his own teachers had guided him into a love of science and math, and that these early lessons that led to his success, in life and on that mission. There was no way without IBM's help Jim Lovell would have been there. He was there that week to work with IBM.

Bob Ballard, the oceanographer, who discovered the Titanic, spoke to all the assembled teachers in a live video conference, from the Woods Hole Oceanographic Institute. He indicated that a decision had been made, that a teacher from Owego's only high school would be traveling with him to the Galapagos Islands and would be broadcasting video via a live satellite feed to each of the schools in the county, for a two week period covering his scientific expedition there, that she would interview the scientists and share he results of their work.

The results of the Eggxspres" experiment was announced, the lab reports were given to the teachers to bring back to their students, and the day concluded.

Would that kind of experience change the way students looked at science? Would more students be more powerfully invited into science and math study?

Do you think the customers were delighted?

Is that how you remember school?

# # #

As you can see startling the customer is not business as usual. If it can be done in the public school, it can be done anywhere. We will share with you one more example from Fran's tenure in Owego about a public school application using this critical principle, hoping that it stimulates a creative approach for you, in startling your customers with extraordinary service.

When Fran went to Owego, eleven students had died in each of the previous eleven years, one per year, in incidents related to drugs and alcohol. Something needed to be done to change the culture among parents and students, to literally to change the current expectations, which were that high school students would, of course, drink and would probably use drugs.

Fran had recently come from New Hampshire, as Superintendent of Schools in Conway. A small town in nearby Maine had lost a group of students in a car-train crash following their graduation ceremony. The crash had probably involved students and alcohol. The community had resolved to never let this happen again. They would create a non-alcohol graduation celebration, so compelling that students would want to celebrate together safely, rather than to use alcohol. Fran was fully aware of the efforts of that community when he faced Owego's problem.

In Owego, the biggest night for drinking and driving was probably the senior prom. The adult community in Owego was very interested in its children. They were very willing to help. Fran approached the service clubs in Owego and found great support from the Rotary, Kiwanis, Elks, Zonta, and the Lions. In order to get students to participate in a post-prom, drug and alcohol free celebration, powerful incentives were needed. Because of the financial contributions from the service organizations, Fran was able to offer a drawing at the end of the post-prom party for an automobile, as an incentive to lure students to attend the event and forgo the traditional bad behavior, and use of alcohol. With the help of the senior high PTA, and a wonderful high school staff, an evening like no other was planned for the students.

A local university gym complex, complete with a dance studio, a pool, racket ball courts, volleyball and basketball courts, was rented out. Students who wished to attend, had to travel to the event on a school bus (no bottles smuggled in), and had to agree to spend the night, enjoying each others company, in safety. The Elks cooked breakfast in the morning, and the students were released to go home, in the broad daylight. The last event of the night was the drawing which included computers, dorm sized refrigerators, dorm size TV's, dictionaries and Thesaurus, and the car. Everyone who attended won something.

When the event was offered to the students, they were slow to sign up. "My parents can't make me do this. It's my right to get drunk, and with any luck do other things, on my prom night," seemed to be the attitude of the students. One week before the event, however, there was virtually no one left among the student body to invite to a non-authorized private and drinking post-prom party. Virtually all students had signed up.

The adults who supervised the event were given a new paradigm. They could not stand around the side of the room in suits and dresses observing (snoopervising), but were required to join in, swimming, playing basketball and even dancing. The focus of the evening was to be entirely based upon fun. No corners were cut. It was a night to remember. Fran wanted the kind of word of mouth advertising that would bring in the students the next year.

# # #

The story doesn't end here. The Chem-Free Prom Party that was offered in Owego was the first in New York State and was a huge success. School districts from across the State came to Owego to learn how to do it. The New York State Assembly asked Fran to testify at a hearing in Albany. Fran did not go alone but brought three students and a local official by the name of Ed Van der Mark. On the way home, one of the students said, "I wish we could do this, all year, instead of just one night." The project that emerged, in Owego, and a number of other districts, was called the "Chem-Free Year". Here's the way the project worked.

Fran recruited some prominent local adults. From year to year the adults changed, but they included the Police Chief, the Mayor, a kindergarten teacher, the principal, a doctor, and others. Then he recruited some key students from the senior class. They also changed from year to year, but they included popular skateboarders, members of a popular garage band, the captain of the football team, the President of the Student Government.

Together with the adults and the students, Fran entered every senior classroom (focusing on English classes). He challenged the students in the classroom, in this manner, "I am not going to drink or use drugs this year. Neither are the other adults and students standing before you. I have $40,000 to spend to provide an outrageous trip or experience every month for those of you who choose to join me in this challenge. We will go skiing, probably more than once, and when we do, the lift ticket is free to you. The ski rentals are free, and a lesson, too. If you are hungry, dinner will be provided... Those of you, who join us, will also go to Toronto or New York City, your choice, for the weekend and, well, you tell us what you want to do. We will try to make it happen."

"If you join, your name is going on a shirt, that you will be given, that will list all the members of the Chem-Free Project, because we mean business. Everyone will know that you signed up. If you cheat, someone will find out. You will have to quit."

"Don't sign up if you don't really want to do this. Don't worry about your parents. We are telling you, before we are telling them. And, if, you want to tell them that that jerk, Murphy didn't let you know about it, and you missed the sign-up date, I'll back your story up. We are kind of hoping you don't join. I've got $40,000 and if you don't sign up, we are all going to Paris. If you do sign up, we will have to split the money more ways, but, I promise you we will have an outrageous year together and your participation will be the stuff that legends are made of."

They sure did sign up in droves. By and large, they kept their word. Subsequent surveys of student drug and alcohol behavior showed a dramatic decline in drug and alcohol behavior among seniors. When the seniors stopped using drugs and alcohol, younger students found it harder to obtain these substances. Drug and alcohol behavior among all students began to decline over a couple of years, when compared to previous years, and when compared to neighboring districts.

More importantly, the students and the volunteer adults had a "ball". Fran remembers distinctly lying on his back in a middle of field in the dark of night in the Catskill Mountains in a huge circle of people lying on their backs heads nearly touching, feet pointing out of the circle, looking at the stars. What a moment!

Most importantly during the time of the project, which went on after Fran left there, and for many years after, Owego lost no more children to deaths related to drugs and alcohol.

Drug and alcohol behaviors among people are not casual behaviors, easily changed. To decide not to use drugs and alcohol, requires the same kind of personal reorganization as losing weight, or developing an exercise program, or turning a non-student into a scholar. The sub-text in both of these stories about the Chem-Free Projects is extraordinary customer service. We have to startle the students with extraordinary treatment that they did not, nor, could not, expect.

Schools do things on the cheap. ("We've got a field trip today to the museum. Bring two dollars for the bus, a dollar for the museum admission and have your mother pack a sandwich.")

These projects would not have worked if students had to pick up responsibility for the costs. They would not have worked if the meal provided did not exceed students' expectations. If the activity was bowling, and not skiing, students may not have done it. (Bowling is something they could do on their own. If the site for the Chem-Free Prom was the high school gym, no one would have come.

How different from or similar to were the style considerations, in the program to reduce drugs and alcohol, than Chrysler's thinking, when they focused on cup holders. How important is it to delight the customer even when, as a public school system, you really are a monopoly.

If schools were to behave like this in all areas, what would happen to student performance? What would happen to taxpayer's support? What would happen to the morale of the staff?

Organizations have to work very hard to startle their customers with customer service. It almost always requires a team. The solutions are always "out-of-the-box" and the work, when done well, turns a company, a store, a school, a government agency, a hospital, a military unit, or a church into a legend.

Scott Shablak, Assistant Dean of Education at Syracuse University, talks about great leaders having three characteristics: grace, legacy, and vision. If you have the vision to startle your customers with the quality of your service and the grace to do it with style, your legacy will be assured.

# # #

T — Test your idea against the facts.

This is a simple step but we need to remember to do it. When Chrysler began to advance the cup holder they had a good idea. My mini van has now at least eight, now.. When does an optimal number of cup holders becomes "transoptimal"?

The President of the Smithsonian Association wrote an interesting article in the Smithsonian Magazine about ten years ago. He talked about "transoptimal" technology. His example was the wrist watch. Fran collects watches.

The first watch was a clock you could carry in your pocket. It wasn't very different from other clocks except, in its size. People who used them carried them in their pocket. Unfortunately, the glass crystals covering the face of the watch would break. So someone invented, what was called the "Hunter's Case", which incorporated a metal cover that would spring open to allow you to see the time. This worked pretty well. These pocket watches were often called Railroad Watches because timing the railroad, at a time when there was one track, east and west, was, often, a life and death matter. Failure to keep proper time would cause "head-on" collisions. These collisions were avoided because the east bound train would pull over on a 'siding" to allow the west bound train to pass. Watches were a big deal for railroad employees and people noted that.

When the Industrial Revolution and mass production began to roll in the early 1900's the pocket watch became less useful. The assembly line worker couldn't take time from his drill press to retrieve the watch from his pocket, pop open the case and read the time. The wrist watch achieved popularity. The worker could turn their wrist, look down, and....

After the advent of solid state technology, the wrist watch changed. For an inexpensive price, a person could buy a wrist watch whose face was totally black. If the person pressed the button on the top of the watch, a set of red numbers would appear indicating the correct time. The President of the Smithsonian Association immediately knew that this technology would not last. The watches were cheap and reliable but he knew that, with this technological advance, we had gone beyond the optimal functioning of a wrist watch and actually walked backwards. It now took two hands to tell the time, again. This was a new dinosaur looking different. It had all the weaknesses of the "railroad watch" with the hunter's case.

Not all advancement is advancement. You can bring a product to the point where the enhancement decreases the likelihood of sale. Would 12 cup holders be helpful in a seven passenger van? If your head rest could include a cup holder, would you want it? You shouldn't guess at customer requirements, needs or desires. You should test the market. Service enhancements are not service enhancements, unless your customer would want them.

Customer service behavior also involves the case of resolving conflicts with customers. How do you use the "test" concept in resolving customer problems? This, too, is pretty simple. The danger here to, is that, if you miss this step, you may fail to resolve the problem.

> Sid loves to go to Romano's Macaroni Grill (they have great customer service). One time, both of us, were eating at the Macaroni Grill. Sid had ordered their lobster ravioli. They were out of the product. He made a second selection, but not without grumbling a little bit. The waiter was great. He apologized. He made suggestions for a tasty alternative and really made Sid feel special.

> We were done with our meal and dessert was in the air. Sid loves Macaroni Grill's Tirimisu. He ordered it. The waiter indicated that he really regretted having to say this twice in one day to a customer. But, they were out of it, too. It was college graduation weekend in Rochester, the crowds were huge, he was sorry. Sid ordered coffee instead.

> Minutes later the manager came over to apologize again. He indicated that he had heard the whole sad story and that he was prepared to offer Sid any item from the dessert menu free of charge to compensate him for his disappointment. Sid said, "You don't have to do that. I am all right."

> Sid doesn't like anything else on the dessert menu.

As we drove away from the restaurant, we realized that this very well meaning manager had actually caused himself a bigger problem, than what he had, when Sid was talking to the waiter.

Sid had actually resolved his problem with Macaroni Grill. When the manager offered something special, Sid was forcefully reminded that he was probably owed compensation for the twin disappointments that evening. But, what he was offered was something he didn't want, and, therefore, for the first time that evening he had felt he had been wronged.

It is a mistake for us to assume that we know our customers well enough to know how to compensate them for any damage or loss they may have experienced due to some problem in our organization. We always have to "test" our solution on the customer before we roll it out.

This should not be confused with a negotiation. Let me show you in the following example how the manager could have done this. Then I will show you the wrong way, or how it might become a negotiation, which would not work.

> "Sid, do you like other things on our dessert menu?" the manager might ask.

> "No", Sid might reply

> "Let me offer you a certificate good for a tirimusu for the next time you come in. I am going to write right on this, that if we are out next time, I will make it double or nothing. If we are out, you will get dinner and dessert", the manager might add.

That was done right. The manager checked to see if he could solve the problem now at the price he was willing to pay, if he couldn't, he already knew Sid loved the tiramisu. He could just offer future opportunities.

Here it is done wrong, as a negotiation:

> "Sid, I like to make this up to you. Would another dessert on the menu be all right?" "No", Sid might reply...".How about a free dinner? How about your first born child? A new Mercedes? A Lear jet?"

You don't ask the customer how much they should be compensated for the loss they have experienced. You ask them which $3.95 choice they would prefer.

This is how you test to make sure your resolution to a conflict with a customer is appropriate.

# # #

0 — Originality and humor help here.

In the beginning of this section of the book, we stressed that diffusing difficult situations, with angry customers, through the reframing approach, requires a sparkle in one's eye. Sid has a great, positive, personality and he rarely is a problem customer, but, all of us have our moments.

> One time Sid was in a difficult situation in a health care environment and he had "lost it". The nurse got a big grin on her face, reached over, and pinched one of Sid's abundant cheeks.
>
> "Aw, poor baby," she said laughingly.
>
> Her laugh allowed this comment to work. It could not and would not have worked otherwise.

# # #

Often what works to deal with customers in a problem situation, can work for you as a customer.

> Recently, Sid was going to a hotel after a very busy day. He had reserved a non-smoking room. When he called the desk, on his way to the hotel, they told him there had been an error in the computer, and, they had reserved him smoking room instead. He was not happy.
>
> When he arrived at the hotel, Sid left his bags in the car, burst through the double doors in the lobby, looking over his shoulders furtively.

"Young lady," he spurted urgently. "Forty three customers are just climbing off my bus in the parking lot. They are tired. They are hungry. And, my, oh my, are they irritable."

"Forty-three people....?" the clerk inquired open mouthed.

"Well, it really is forty-four. We reserved a room for me, too. Now, they are all single rooms and all non-smoking. I've got the reservation receipt right here." He fumbled through his briefcase.

"But ...", she stammered.

"Just kidding." Sid smiled.

She laughed, relieved that she was not going to have find rooms for forty-four, hungry, tired, and irritable people. This drama introduced by Sid was a real high point in her evening. She would tell it to others, at home, later.

"Now that I am the person that saved you from that horrible fate, can't you find me just one non-smoking room?" Sid asked. "I am tired, irritable and hungry. Look how easy this problem is. There is only one of me, not forty four."

The desk clerk placed Sid in a suite, at no additional charge, that was non-smoking.

His originality and humor got him something that he would not otherwise have.

This situation with Sid started with the *caution* that he was facing a difficult situation with this clerk. It went through the *understanding* that she probably had a few high end rooms in reserve. He *startled* her with a fresh approach.

In this case, he was only going to get one chance to resolve this problem, so the only *test* he could employ was to test this in his mind. Then he rolled it out with *originality* and humor.

To some people, reframing seems a little like teasing. It really is simply a way to help people find their own common humanity in a situation. All of us have had the problem of a computer glitch that has caused us to miss an opportunity. If we can find the humor in it, and find our common experience, we probably will treat each other well, even in a difficult situation. The clerk was just playing an old tape. It probably runs something like this: "Those fools in data processing, can't they get anything right? Here is another angry customer. I hate this. I am going to have to disappoint him again. This job stinks. I will just have to grin and bear it.'

When Sid reframes the problem, she begins to see him differently and the problem differently. She appreciates the humor and is willing to "go to bat" for this guy who treats her the way her older brother does. It is this last point that makes it seem a little like teasing someone.

There is power in this model. People who use it break down the barriers between "us" and "them". When those barriers disappear, the "us" and "them" becomes "we" and "us". When it is just "us", we can usually resolve the problem.

Let's use this model, one more time, from a customer service perspective.

> A long time ago Johnson and Evenrude Motors manufactured a device that was used for skin diving. It was a floating compressor unit that pumped air through a twenty-five foot hose to the "diver" below. Johnson called theirs the air buoy unit.

> The units were discovered to be defective. Sooner or later the exhaust manifold would crack and exhaust would get into the air intake valve. Fran had been using his device for about eight years when the exhaust manifold cracked. Smoke began to enter his face mask and put his life at risk. He did not know about the problem with the design. (He had bought it used and was not on a "recall" list from the company.) When he brought it in to be repaired, the shop told him they could not repair it. The company would not permit it. These devices were too dangerous.

> In those days, there was no remedy. Johnson and Everude were not compelled to make it right. And, they did not. The only option available to the dealer was to suggest to Fran, the customer, that he take this relatively expensive piece of equipment to the curb. This was not a good answer from Fran's perspective.

The argument went on long and hard. There was no apparent solution in sight. In those days, the dealer had few options to address the problem. Finally, the dealer said in frustration, "All right, I'll replace it. I'll give you an equivalent value to this product in pounds of arsenic."

"What would I do with arsenic? It would kill me," Fran muttered.

"Ah Ha", the dealer smiled. "You are beginning to catch on." I can't use that broken machine either, we are both victims here.

This did not completely resolve the problem, of course, but, at least both parties shared one common insight and had enjoyed some laughter together, which, was not a bad beginning.

The approach of the dealer, in this case, showed _originality_ and held within it the possibility of humor.

When designing customer service standards and expectations, _originality_ is also important. People are not going to satisfy today's customers with a level of service they find all around them. Today's customers expect a fresh, _original_ level of service, not a warmed over approach borrowed from the company XYZ.

If you have done your research and you understand the customer's relationship or potential relationship with your product or service, you have the chance to create a truly _original_ concept. Fran was Superintendent of Schools in Conway, New Hampshire. During his time there, there were 7,500 local residents; yet, on any given weekend, there could be 75,000.

The 75,000 justified a movie theatre, but the 7500 did not. The theatre took a page from the ski area's play book. The movie theatre was under-utilized during the week and packed on the weekends. They offered a mid-week annual pass. If people bought the pass at $200 a year per family, or $50 per person, they could come as many times as they wanted, Sunday through Thursday. (They offered the passes for sale in November and December, to make it a convenient Holiday present.)

The movie theatre maximized use of their mid-week capacity and dramatically increased revenues. They delighted the low paid local residents, who could suddenly afford to go to the movies frequently. It was a "win-win".

Originality was a natural out-growth of the understanding that was developed about its customers. Local residents loved the pass. This kind of originality often delights the customer.

M — Make it non-confrontational

This is an example of what reframing is not:

Thank God, it was an unseasonably warm day when a timid young Alice signed up for a ski lesson with Sven. It took 20 minutes to help Alice put her ski boots in the binding on the skis. (It usually took 5 minutes) It took five unsuccessful trials for her to finally master getting on the ski lift to go to the top of the easy slope. Her immobility at the top of the hill lasted another twenty minutes and it took her two hours to come down the first 400 yards.

Another ski instructor flashed by Sven and Alice while they paused at the top of the hill to start their second run.

'That's what I would like to do!" Alice said hopefully.

Svan replied, "When pigs fly!"

He thought he had reframed the situation

What he had done, of course, was to use his old habit of sarcasm, but call it reframing. It was, of course, still the old sarcasm.

Reframing is aimed at a "win-win". When reframing has been done successfully, both sides are smiling, feeling happy and positive, a problem has been put into a new context. There is some relief in that both sides will not have to wallow in a difficult problem. Clarity has been gained from ambiguity.

When it goes very badly, someone tries to "win", someone tries to put someone else down, using sarcasm and calling it reframing. This approach never succeeds, and, in fact, can bring a negative reaction.

Reframing is never designed to defeat the customer.

Sid is a natural at reframing because of the twinkle in his eyes. He clearly shows he is joking with you, not making fun of you.

E — Exercise your risk-taking.

Any new behavior is a risk taking behavior. Repeated patterns of behavior tend to bring repeated results. If someone was accustomed to using a snow shovel to shovel my driveway, they pretty much know what to expect. They know how long it will take. They know how stiff their back will be. They know how high the piles of snow will become after they shovel the snow. They can even imagine how heavy each shovel will be, depending on the temperature outside.

If someone buys them a new snow blower, all that predictability goes out the window. They now, cannot predict anything.

The snow blower will be a great improvement but they are taking a risk. Predictability builds confidence. When things are predictable, they are reliable. When they cannot be predicted they are unreliable.

Most of us would view the new snow blower as a plus. But, there is some risk in changing.

All change requires some level of risk. Bobby Kennedy said, "Change is not neutral, change has enemies."

In order to try reframing, we need to try new behaviors. Sid and Fran can use reframing with less risk. They have been doing it for years. There is significant risk with reframing. If you try to use reframing and you dip into sarcasm, your customer will see your behavior as confrontational, and their tendency to be defensive will actually increase. You definitely need to be optimistic with a sparkle in your eye in order to have reframing safely.

Exercise is a good way to think about this. We don't encourage people to jump right into reframing with customers without any practice. Just like in exercise, you should start slowly, safely, and increase, as your "muscles" get stronger. Here are some practical suggestions of how to begin and how to grow in your ability to help others reframe safely:

- Begin using reframing as a customer. The people you are doing business with can't afford to punch you in the nose or holler at you, if it goes badly. They get paid to be nice to you. Therefore, these are particularly safe people to use to try your new skills out on.

- Try it among your family and friends.

- Try the simple ones like a fresh answer to a simple question like "How are you today?"

- When you bring it to the work place, try it first with subordinates and colleagues.

- When your colleagues discover what you are doing, role-play with them how you might use it to deal with difficult customers. Practice until every body agrees you have got it right.

- When you are feeling comfortable, reframe some issues for your boss.

- Now you are ready to try it on your customers. Begin gently. Watch for feedback. Expand your risk taking, as you find success.

If you have done it right, people will find you to be a funny person, with a fresh perspective. They will think their experience with you has been fun. They will tell others, that you "Made their day".

R — Roll it Out

Why would we "roll it out"? The truth is that in spite of all this talk about a service economy, the expectation for customer service is steadily climbing while service itself is disappearing. Our encounters with businesses today inevitably bring us disappointments. More and more restaurants expect me to get my own food and bus my own tables. Gone are the knowledgeable department stores and hardware stores where true experts would talk knowledgeably about the products and offer solid advice prior to purchase. What we find instead are warehouses with cash registers.

Shoe stores, for example, used to be places that measured your feet and brought you their products to try. Now you are faced with an acre of shoe racks and a cash register.

Customer service is at an all time low.

The approach to customers today, too often, also fails to meet the mark. Customers get into our face. We fall into comfortable, defensive patterns. The situation escalates, and everyone goes home with elevated blood pressure, unhappy.

Clearly, we need to rethink customer relations at two levels. First, we need to focus on how we can delight the customer. How can our product or service become indispensable to our customer? How can we set a new standard for service for our customer that puts competitive products or services, at competitive disadvantage? In order to do this, we must reframe our own thinking. We must create startling new goods or services that reflect a profound understanding of our customer's needs, wants, and desires.

Second, we need to find a way to resolve the inevitable conflicts that will arise from the disappointments that our customers have in our goods and services. In order not to fall into the old traps of defensive behavior, we need to reframe these encounters to help our customers find our common interests and values. We need to startle these customers with fresh approaches and embrace them with our concern and support.

Motivation and Enthusiasm

Teachers often complain about unmotivated students. "If these kids were motivated to learn, I could teach them a ton." Employers often talk about unmotivated employees. "They are just plain, not motivated to excellence."

Most psychologists agree that people are born motivated. Babies are motivated to eat. (Ask any nursing mother.) They are motivated to sleep, go to the bathroom, be held, etc. In fact motivational problems with children are not usually identified until they enter school.

"I was king of the hill, apple of my mother's eye, leader of my chums until I met you, teacher, and all your words and numbers."

A researcher named Seligman began a direction in psychological research that has really helped us understand what happens to motivation. Seligman was studying dogs in a cage with a shoulder high barrier dividing the cage into two sides. . There was an electric grid under each side of the cage. It was an old and familiar experiment. (We are not endorsing the apparent cruelty of this experiment, but it was done. Let's us learn from it.)

A light would come on and fifteen seconds later the side of the cage where the dog was standing when the light went on would get a jolt of electricity. If the dog had not learned to leap over to the safe side, the dog would get a shock.

The good news for dogs in this kind of experiment is that dogs learned to leap to the safe side of the cage after only about 15 trials. Seligman's experiment was different. He chained the dog to the unsafe side of the cage. He gave the dog fifteen shocks, and then released it to move freely about the cage. After 70 trials, the dogs still had not learned to leap to the safe side of the cage.

The behaviors of each of the dogs were unique. Some dogs defecated. Some dogs vomited. Some dogs shook. But, whatever behavior the dog exhibited, they would continue that behavior each time the light went on instead of seeking a behavior that brought them relief. The only way the dogs could be taught to get to the safe side of the cage, when the light came on, was to drag them with long leaches to the safe side of the cage until they learned the pattern and moved on their own. But, this only worked when the barrier in the middle was removed. Seligman called the underlying behavioral deficit, "Learned Helplessness."

Seligman said that when a person or an animal is placed in a situation where there is no alternative but failure they sometimes learn that their own skilled behavior cannot get the results they seek. Their persistence at task declines and, their ability to find successful behavior in that task was compromised.

There have been thousands of studies using people and animals that have confirmed this finding. Learned helplessness is a stable concept in the "new" psychology.

The studies on people have been less cruel but very interesting. One psychologist asked students to do complicated academic work in an environment that had loud uncontrollable noise. There were three groups. One group had the noise and could do nothing about it. Another group had no noise at all. The third group had a button in the room that they were told they could use to lower the noise, if they needed to (The button was, in fact, not connected to anything.) They were asked not to use it. They were given the same noise as the first group and were asked to do the same tasks as the other groups.

The first group did poorly on their academic tasks. They were, after all, much like the dogs in Seligman's original experiment "chained" to and inescapable negative circumstance. The group that had no noise at all, of course, did pretty well. The surprise was that the group that thought they could control the noise (even though they couldn't) performed about as well as the group that had no noise at all.

One of the amazing findings the psychologist found in this experiment was that they students in the uncontrollable noise group did significantly less well on an unrelated academic test, back in their regular classroom, during the next week. It appears that the effects of being chained to a negative circumstance extend outward to other non-related, life events.

In plain English, the facts are these, when people believe that bad things are going to happen to them and there is nothing to do to prevent it, they become unmotivated and dysfunctional. This probably should not surprise us, if we think about it.

In the circumstance where a loved one dies, we find ourselves chained to a negative circumstance. We try new doctors for a second option. We search the Internet for new medicines. We try macrobiotic diets. No matter what we do, the person dies. Here we are chained, just like in the earlier experiments, our persistence at tasks declines and we become, at least, temporarily dysfunctional. Human reactive depression, (the most common form of every day depression) Seligman holds, may be the same thing as Learned Helplessness.

The plain and simple fact is that unmotivated people are easy to find; we can manufacture them. In fact, we do. When a teacher demands that a student do something that they cannot physically accomplish, like learn to read, when their eyes are not physically developed, the teacher manufactures a student who will carry with themselves, a lifetime of poor motivation. This is not overstated. Research supports this statement. Young minds are like fresh poured concrete. When you drop something on them, it often makes an impression.

We can do this to employees and customers as well. Perhaps the impact will not be as profound or long lasting as it will be on children, at home, and in school, but the impact will be longer lasting and more profound then we might, at first, think.

An example of how an employer destroyed the motivation of an employee happened recently in a store in the Rochester area. A night cleaner that had had a lot of experience in the janitorial field was upgraded from a buffer to a high-speed buffer to clean his floors. He knew that the high speed buffer required a different kind of wax. He knew this because of his previous experience working in other companies and because he spoke to the representative from the floor wax company and the representative from the buffers. Many of his friends worked as janitors. He knew his profession. He mentioned to his boss that the high-speed buffer, with the old product, would cause the floors to be milky or cloudy because the increased friction of the high-speed buffer would burn the old wax.

He was told, "We are going to continue to use the old product. It has always worked well for us."

He continued to raise the issue and continued to get the same feedback. He showed his supervisor the "milky" floors, and could not capture his boss's attention to the problem. As time went on, he began to take less interest in his work. The way he framed the problem was, "If they don't care how this place looks, why should I?"

The cleanliness of the store declined. The business declined. He was fired, because his boss said, "He is a lazy good for nothing." The business closed. Even though a new cleaner temporarily improved the cleanliness of the building, the reputation of this food store had gotten so low that the customers never came back.

Employees are often paired with inescapable negative circumstances by bosses who don't listen. Except in rare circumstances the employee is the greatest expert about their own job. The secretary knows more about her job than the boss does. Why wouldn't the boss listen to the secretary, as she explains her need for equipment, materials or training?

Customers, too, can be made dysfunctional. In ways that businesses don't often understand, they establish relationships with customers. Many employees see customer encounters as events, not relationships. For the customer, it is not a string of unrelated events, but a relationship.

Let us share with you, first, a good example. Dave, who runs his own barbershop in the Browncroft neighborhood in Rochester, knows he shares a relationship with his customers. People who have lived in that neighborhood, sometimes, 20 years apart, can connect with each other by laughing about their experiences with

Dave, the barber. Dave is funny and warm. He never forgets a face or a person's story. His shop is filled with strangers and friends who rapidly become friends caught in the embrace of Dave's laughter. Dave becomes so captured in the stories at his shop that every once in awhile the hair cut is a dud.

What is interesting is how David empowers his customers.

"David, I'm OK with this hair cut but my wife told me that it is ridiculous. She says it is shaggy on the right and short on the left," a recent customer said.

"Did you get out of the chair before I was done? Doggone it, you are always doing that. Spin around here. Show these guys that hair cut. What do you guys think? I could never have done this, could I? Sit down in this chair. Let me finish this one up...and, next time, don't be in such a hurry to get out of here. Be sure to tell your wife what a jerk you are. Don't blame this one on the old David. And, next time don't be so quick to get out of here."

All of us in the barbershop knew that if we had a problem with a haircut, no muss, no fuss. He empowered us through this example, as customers, to raise our concerns. He showed us that this was a relationship where one could feel free to raise issues.

By contrast, there is a car dealership in that same neighborhood that never makes a mistake. When the newly installed battery ran out of power within the first month, they asked the customer what he had done to it. When a car being serviced, was vandalized, in their lot, they said it was his problem. When the car would not start and they first fixed X, and the car still didn't start, they fixed Y, then Z and charged for all three; they taught the customer to stop raising concerns, to have the prestige of doing business with the dealer. Some customers, however, simply learned to go elsewhere.

No customer will be an interactive customer sharing concerns and seeking improvements if they are chained to a hostile or non-responsive company. They will either quit complaining or they will leave. Both responses are fatal to a company committed to continuous improvement.

# # #

The flip side of motivation is accomplished when one looks at what motivates customers instead of what makes them dysfunctional. The same researcher, Martin Seligman has recently published some very interesting new materials. He has been able to predict elections based on the optimism of the candidates. He has been able to predict the winners of athletic competitions based upon the optimism of the players and coaches in newspaper accounts following their previous victories and defeats. The results of his research on elections show clearly what other research also reveals that people are attracted to positive, enthusiastic, and upbeat people.

Try this. I am going to introduce you to two women. The first is Sally. The second is Mary.

Sally believes life is difficult. A frequent topic of conversation is her aliments and her friends' ailments. She frequently complains about taxes, her child's teachers, the cost of living, and the government. Her instant response to a proposal for anything, from anybody, is to say no. She walks with a stoop and has fairly low energy. On the plus side, she is loyal, long-suffering and is very interested in other peoples' tales of woe.

Mary believes life is good. She is always looking ahead to the next challenge, and opportunity. She is full of energy, seldom complains about anything, and always likes to say yes to any hair-brained idea that has any possibility to bring good results. In the darkest situation, she can find something to feel good about. She has little patience with other people's sad stories and always wants to do something new, get something done, and move ahead. She is very future focused and doesn't like to spend a lot of time on the past.

OK, here is the challenge. You are going to Cleveland for a conference. The weather will be rainy. You are going to spend a lot of time with one of these two employees. Mary or Sally. Who do you want to go with?

The fact is that 90% by actual account of the people we ask this question to, choose Mary.

Enthusiasm and optimism makes a huge difference to our customers, our colleagues and our employees. (Even to us?)

Optimism and enthusiasm are a choice. We all have about the same number of bad things happen to us. (Sure, some of us have it a little tougher.) Generally, we will all be born, establish relationships, some of which will succeed and some of which will fail. We will all lose friends and relatives to illness and death. We will all have successes and failures and we will all get sick and die. Generally. These are not the real issues. In fact, some of the most cheerful people that I know have been in wheelchairs or have had cancer. The question is not how much bad stuff has happened to each of us. The question is how have we responded to it.

How much pleasure does misery brings us? Some people seem to revel in it. Do we choose the misery button?

Let's play it out. On Friday night, one of our parents was diagnosed with cancer. On Saturday night, one of our pre-teen children came home drunk. It is Monday. A customer calls on a phone. Will our lives be enriched by being gruff or unkind to that customer, or is there a possibility that by extraordinarily helpful to the customer, our lives may be more enriched?

# # #

It is important to charge your batteries. At a meeting Sid will often ask, "How many of you like herbal tea?" Not very many hands go up. Sid indicates that he understands. He says that he usually makes himself a cup of it in the morning when he is in the office. People come by his desk and as him, "Sid, you are going to drink that tea before it gets cold?"

Sid's response? "Nope."

The questioner often looks at him peculiarly.

"I'm not going to drink this tea. I hate herbal tea. But, I sure do like how it smells," he says.

Sid works at charging his batteries, so does Fran. You must, as well. Being kind to others requires that you first be kind to yourself. Glasser, in his famous book <u>Reality Therapy</u> contends that people have four basic needs:

- They have a need for achievement. They need to make or do important things.

- They have a need for power. They have to feel that they can influence or control people, events, or things in their environment.

- They have a need for affiliation. They have a need to belong, to love and be loved. They have to feel that people around them care about them.

- They have a need for fun. They have to be able to play, relax, laugh and enjoy.

If the organization won't permit or encourage people to satisfy these needs, Glasser says, they will find a way to do it themselves. Sometimes, they will solve it in a way that is hostile to the organization.

In an organization that does not permit play, (a strict seventh grade class, for example,) people will find an opportunity to play, sometimes with sarcasm, sometimes in a malicious way, sometimes with vandalism. How are you satisfying your four needs? How is your organization encouraging people to satisfy these four needs?

Do you find an opportunity to play every day? Do you "play" with your customers, your colleagues, your bosses? Do you ever organize opportunities, where you work, for people to play? Golf tournaments, for example, song contests, boss look-alike contests, parties, surprises. Could you recharge your customers and yourself with silly promotions and games?

Dave, the barber, could recharge himself and his customers by issuing clipboards and crayons with a challenge to draw Dave, the barber, as he looked in the sixties, and then show them a photo. The photo would reveal that this civilizer of men's hair once looked like an unkempt hippy.

Play should be an important way that we recharge our customers and ourselves.

Achievement can recharge us too. For those of us who are bosses, it is important for us to remember to share the positives we get from achieving a big goal. If the goal is achieved by the boss, alone, in the report at the end of the project, then he or she is the only person who gets to experience the achievement.

It is recognition that makes achievement possible. Customers can be recognized for loyalty, their twenty-fifth visit, their good ideas, (cash prizes for suggestions realized), and other contributions. A jeweler we know gives particularly cheerful customers a card thanking them for making his day.

Affiliation can recharge people's batteries. Fran teaches, in his classes, at the college, that one of the most important tips for improving time management is to spend at least 15 minutes a day at work, without an agenda, with someone you genuinely like. He has observed in his own professional practice that when he makes it a point to do this, each day, he is more energetic and focused and can accomplish more. Dave, the barber, will spend anywhere from eight to 20 minutes cutting a person's hair. When he is cutting the hair of someone he really likes, and there is no crowd in his shop, he will deliberately slow down and enjoy the time he is spending with the customer. It recharges him for the rest of his customers.

Power, too, recharges us. The funny thing about power is that the more you share it, the more of it you have. The boss who empowers her employees gets more respect and power from them. One boss we know said to her employee, "That's a very good problem that you have raised; I like the way you are thinking about it. I trust you to resolve it satisfactorily. Why don't you go ahead and make the decision on that?" She empowered the employee. The employee derived a boost from her boss' confidence that gave her more energy that day.

We can do this with customers, too. Nothing is more empowering to a customer than to say, " Great suggestion, we will implement it next week."

People really do have basic and fundamental needs. Ignoring your customers' needs will cause an inappropriate expression of them somewhere else. Supporting the needs will provide a release from the cares at hand and a boost for the employee or customer.

One of the women who approached Sid after a seminar told him that she treats herself well every day. She puts out the good china when she makes tea for herself on a weekend afternoon. She does not anticipate company, or guests. She brings out the nice napkins. She does not put the tea bag in the cup but prepares the tea in the "special" teapot that her mother gave her.

"That's really nice," Sid remarked. "Why do you do that?"

"I have had some bad news recently," the woman replied.

"How is that?" Sid inquired

"I have a terminal disease. The doctors told me that there is not much they can do for me, except to put me in touch with people who could help me cope with what I am going through. I didn't use their experts. I just decided to treat myself really well. Sometimes I wear that special nightgown that I had put away for a really special evening, just for me. I pour a glass of wine and light some candles. I really work hard on the little things. I am much more conscious of using the time I have, well."

Our time is always transitory. We don't have the luxury of knowing when our last day is. What are we waiting for? Why wouldn't we treat ourselves as a guest? Are we not guest in our own life?

Each of us needs to be fresh. We need to be fresh for our children, our spouses or significant others, our friends, our colleagues, and, oh yes, our customers. Being fresh is not an accident. In order to be fresh we need to refresh. We should not rely entirely on others to be treated well. We should carefully build our own mood.

Sid and Fran really like good coffee. Spending the extra few dollars a pound or fifty cents a cup to have it done right is an important way for them to acknowledge their own personhood, and refresh themselves.

All of us look forward to a vacation. Some how, a whining customer is easier to tolerate the day before you leave on a vacation to Bermuda. But, we can't go to Bermuda every week. How do we build for ourselves little mental vacations to refresh ourselves every day that we live? Could we learn from the lady who has discovered that she has a terminal disease?

If your contribution to your family, to your colleagues, to your business, to your customers has the potential to be worthy, than it is worthwhile to recharge your batteries for all the other people you help, or have the potential to help. There is far too little patience in our society today. It is easy with the stresses that surround us to be short with other people. Being kind to yourself helps you to be kind to other people.

When a person is hurling down a hill at a high rate of speed, it is not a good time to be discovering where the brake pedal is. This is the time to learn what enriches your life, and makes you happy; not when you are under peak amounts of stress. Take the time now to make a list of those things you will do for yourself to help center yourself. Then do them. Do those things that delight yourself for your family, your friends, your coworkers, and your customers. Now is not too soon.

Empathy should not stop at your front door. It is important that you have empathy for yourself. Meditation is making an appointment with yourself. It is how people get in touch with their issues and who they are.

There are strategic planners who never take the time to plan their own lives and their own careers. There are some systems that people can use to put their own lives in order. Steven Covey is a good source for thinking about these issues. Many of the ideas that follow were inspired by his work.

Well organized people make their calendars the bosses of their life. Time is our only nonrenewable resource. How we spend our time is how we spend our lives. Could you spend your time one way and your life another way? Our impact on our families, our church, our own physical self, our business, and our customers will be determined by how we spend our time. Wouldn't it be a great epitaph on our gravestone to have the words, "A life well spent"?

Yet most of us let others set our calendars for us. With computerized calendar systems, in some organizations, people can literally enter your calendar, set up appointments, and cause you to attend them. This is a felony, time theft.

Time is like money. There is not enough of it and it has too many competing uses. People who are good with money budget it and carefully monitor its use. Is money worth more than time? Should we bring the methods we use to manage money over to how we manage time?

Budgets work when people declare their purposes, and then organize their money to achieve these purposes. The reason we have budgets because there are unlimited demands on money and only a limited resource. Time is same. There are unlimited demands on our time and there is only so much time to go around. In the following section we will provide some tips to help you budget your time so that you can be more effective personally, professionally, and for your customers. The system we will use is a budgeting system.

First, whether it is money or time, people have to be clear about their most important priorities for the scarce resource or it will be spent "Willy-Nilly". The proper use of a calendar is to budget time. This begins with a statement of strategic purposes. In order to follow this process you are going to have to schedule a couple of hours with yourself, then an hour with your boss, then an hour with your immediate friends or family. Here is how you are going to use that time:

- Ask yourself what is the most important effort you need to do for yourself *physically.*

- Ask yourself what is absolutely the most critical activity you need to do for yourself *socially and with your family.*

- Ask yourself what you absolutely must do for yourself *spiritually.*

- Ask yourself what are the most critical steps you should do for yourself *professionally* including what *you need to do for your business and for your customers.*

- Ask yourself what would best develop you and satisfy your needs *intellectually and culturally,*

A self reflective time on this important activity is critical. If you don't know where you are going, any road will take you there. If you are going to make decisions about how you are going to spend your time you had better know what you want to accomplish. How could you better do that, then asking yourself these important questions? The answers will help you find balance among the competing interests for the use of your time.

However, if you are like most of the people that we meet every day, thinking, alone, by yourself, will not bring you the best answers. Most of us need to review our thoughts with others. It would help to review your thoughts about the business and professional objectives with you boss and colleagues. The more personal objectives would, perhaps, best be reviewed with friends and family. Gather other people's ideas. Settle on a clear set of objectives personally and professionally for the next year. Take this work seriously. This is, after all, an effort to determine how you will spend the next year of your life. Sit in front of a fireplace or by a mountain lake. Think long thoughts. Generate too many options. Boil your goals down to seven or fewer. Make sure they include physical, spiritual, social or family, business, and intellectual/cultural goals, unless one or more of these areas is going so well that it does not need improvement. That could happen.

What's this got to do with the use of time? Everything! If time is limited; and it is, then spend time on what is important. What is important? If you haven't taken the time to sort that out, you won't know.

Why did we say this was a budgetary process? Because, it is. The very same goals will help you decide how it is you will spend your money. All effective budgets begin with the establishment of strategic priorities. Without that step, there is no direction or order to the expenditure of funds.

If a calendar is your most important tool to manage your expenditure of time, and if time is the most critical resource, then let's pull our calendars out. Whether they are on a computer, Personal Digital Assistant, or paper, we need to actively use them. They are a tool. People who never bounce a check, reconcile their checkbooks daily or weekly. Here are some steps to use our calendar in a way that acknowledges how critical time is to our personal and professional success:

Tips for time management:

1. Schedule a time on your calendar every week for a minimum of 15 minutes to make mid-course correction on your calendar. Enter that in your calendar now.

2. Take out the goals you have written for yourself; physical, social/emotional, spiritual, your business self, and your intellectual/cultural.

3. Review those goals first during the fifteen minutes you have scheduled each week.

4. Examine the contents of your calendar for the past week. *(Make your calendar accurate by putting everything you do in it (even those things that happen that weren't scheduled.) It is the only way you can study your time use. It is as important as keeping a record of every check in your checkbook.)* Measure your use of time that week against your goals. If those were your goals, how did you use your time?

5. Resolve how you will improve your time use to achieve your goals.

6. Review your calendar for the next week and make adjustments to achieve your goals.

7. Semi-annually re-craft your goals.

People who start poor and become rich don't have that happen to them by accident. People who become wealthy do so by having a relentless focus on wealth. It is certainly not asking too much, if we want to use our time well that we spend 15 minutes a week reviewing our use of time, and that semi-annually we reprioritize

"I have always wanted to write a book," people often say to writers.

"I always wanted run a marathon," some people say to runners.

"Really, what have you done about it," we are tempted to reply.

With all due respect to the religions of the planet and their aspirations for and belief in the afterlife, this is probably the only time we will live this life on this planet. It is not a rehearsal. Let's do it well.

# # #

People often confuse the question of urgency with importance. Let's first define importance. Those things that advance your goals are important. Those things that do not are not important. (This is particularly true when you have tested your goals by sharing them with your boss, and sharing them with your family.

Urgency can be a false importance. It rears its ugly head with the news that this (whatever "this" is) must be done now. However, it can be a charlatan. Urgency often responds to what is important to other people, who's goals may have nothing to do with yours.

You are a school building principal in the following example. A call comes in from a woman who is an artist from out-of-town. She is speaking at a luncheon at the senior citizen center this afternoon and she needs to know right now, will you be there for lunch. They are making the lunch count right now.

How important would you guess this is on your priority as a principal? Yet, it is urgent, at least to the person who comes from out-of-town.

There are several tips that this may not be high on your goals. The artist is from out-of-town. Senior citizens may not be your most important targeted audience.

Please note the chart below.

	Urgent	Not Urgent
Important		
Not Important		

While you are learning the new technique, we would say to put this chart on a big pad on your desk. Make the boxes big enough to pile paper in. When the in-coming mail comes in, or challenges for appointments or tasks to do, resolve them by putting them in the appropriate box. Here is how to use the boxes.

- The urgent and important box is reserved for things you must do right now *(or at least real soon).*

- The important and non-urgent box is reserved for things that you should get to pretty soon. *(They should find their way some place on your calendar today or some definite point in the future to be done as time permits.)*

- The unimportant but urgent should be delegated. *(Let other people deal with the urgency felt by others about things that are not important to you.)* If it isn't important, (and you are a busy person), you should not do it.

- Those things that are both unimportant and not urgent should be placed on the top of a pile in your lower right hand drawer. Every six weeks, you should pull out the bottom third of that pile and throw it away unexamined. *(If no one has noticed it lying unattended in your bottom drawer for six weeks, it probably isn't worth rereading.)* If it is that important to them, they probably kept a copy.) You don't read it before throwing it away, because that is a waste of time.

Most religions believe in a judgment day. We could imagine St. Peter (or his equivalent from other religions) meeting a newcomer at the pearly gates (or its equivalent) to ask the following question, "You have been given 72 years. What have you accomplished?" Maybe that is all you will be held accountable in the end. What else is worth asking?

How you use your time will determine whether you have the time to focus on your customers, to see the issues from their side, and to develop solutions that will delight your customers.

Unless you have your social/emotional (family) life in order; unless you have your physical life in order; unless you have your intellectual/cultural life in order; unless you have your spiritual life in order; you will not have the kind of psychic reserves that are needed to give world class customer service.

The reason they tell you to put the oxygen mask on yourself first, on an airplane, which has lost pressurization, is because you can't help the child sitting next you when you are unconscious. You must first attend to yourself, before you can reliably and cheerfully assist others. Build the time into your life to stretch, relax, and refresh.

# # #

We all want world class customers. We want them to be engaged, happy, excited, and connected to us. We want them to love our service or our product. We strongly believe that people, in contact with the customer, either manufacture world class customers or real cranks.

When Sid says "Put into others what you want back", he is reaffirming a variation of the golden rule which has been taught by nearly all religions and all philosophers since nearly the beginning of recorded time. "Do onto others as you would have them do onto you"

People behave as they themselves are treated. It is hard to treat grandma badly on Thanksgiving Day when she is serving you pie and gazing lovingly into your eyes.

Who is in charge of the results you get from the way you treat others?

Objectively, probably sometimes you are in charge and sometimes not. Which of us controls a lightening bolt, or controls with absolute certainty, a heart attack? Do we really control the person sitting opposite of us? Do we really control the people who report to us? Is there a parent reading this book that believes that they control their child, absolutely (when they are out of sight)?

Yet, some of us harbor the illusion that we do.

Here is what we know about people who believe they are in charge of the results they get:

- They are more successful than people who do not.

- They have greater persistence at task.

- They persevere.

- They report greater happiness from life.

It is an illusion. The truth? We control some things and some things we do not control. But we have a choice, as in most things, about how we choose view our control of others.

Sid and Fran believe strongly that if you believe you can delight your customer by using these simple robust techniques, you will develop customers who are delighted and your personal happiness will increase and your success, as well.

Put into others what you want back. It won't work every time. What does? But....